**979.1 K388c
Kennedy, W.D. "Ar
 Chasing rainbow
similar acts of foolishness**

S0-EWF-779

Chasing Rainbows
And Similar Acts
of Foolishness

Chasing Rainbows And Similar Acts of Foolishness

W.D. "Arizona" Kennedy

Copyright © 2008 by W.D. "Arizona" Kennedy.

ISBN:	Hardcover	978-1-4363-4447-0
	Softcover	978-1-4363-4446-3

All rights reserved. No part of this book may be reproduced or transmitted in any form or by any means, electronic or mechanical, including photocopying, recording, or by any information storage and retrieval system, without permission in writing from the copyright owner.

This book was printed in the United States of America.

To order additional copies of this book, contact:
Xlibris Corporation
1-888-795-4274
www.Xlibris.com
Orders@Xlibris.com

This book is dedicated to the late-great Raymond McCormick, who told me that the only way I would ever make a dollar treasure hunting, would be by writing about it, and to my wife, Cam, who encouraged me to write my life-story. I also want to express my gratitude to my sister, Peggy Atkinson, and to her son Ben, for their tireless efforts in preparing this book for publication.

Volume One

It would be impossible to describe a somewhat uneventful lifetime in any kind of sequence. But I will try to describe some of the events that I remember best.

I was born in the Cochise County Hospital in Douglas, Arizona in 1940, number five in a family of eight. I don't remember much about that event. My parents were Bill and Phyllis Kennedy, and were living on my late (maternal) Grandpa Stoner's place in Hereford, AZ. Grandpa was killed by lightning in 1939. I think we lived there for a year or two, until they could settle the estate, but I'm not sure. When I was a year or two old we moved to a parcel of land on Frontier Road, between Bisbee and Elfrida, in the Sulphur Springs Valley. My Grandma Stoner had homesteaded this land, with the help of Momma and her sister, Mary Rowena, in the late 1920's. She let my folks build a livable home on the south half of her eighty acre homestead. This eighty acre homestead still belongs to several of my siblings, except for one five acre lot which was sold to outsiders.

We lived in the original house until 1952 or 1953, at which time my Daddy, with Momma's help, built the existing house. The lumber that went into building the new house came from Johnson Addition in Bisbee, where homes had to be moved to make way for the Lavender Pit. Daddy made all the adobes that went into the walls out in our back yard. He built this house when he was supposed to be bedridden with a heart attack.

Some of my earliest memories started when I was three or four years old. One of the things I remember was following the turkey hens to their nest and taking their eggs when they had left the nest. We would give the turkey eggs to a banty hen to set and hatch, because the banty hens were better mothers than the turkey hens.

Along about 1943 or 1944, we were out in the yard one day, and saw a couple of boys coming down the road from our grandma's house with a billy goat they had borrowed from her. It was Raymond and Leland McCormick. Leland was riding the goat, and Raymond was leading it. They had a dog that was half coyote tagging along behind. We found out that they lived a couple of miles across the creek from us. Anyhow, this started a friendship that has lasted more than sixty years. We have had a lot of good times together over the years.

We were a large family, and money was pretty scarce, so we had to make our own amusement. I remember how much fun it was to go out and pretend to drive the old Terraplane Hudson car that was sitting up on blocks out in our front yard. It was broke down, and I don't think it ever did get fixed. We probably sold it for junk, or gave it away.

It seems like we always had some kind of music around the house. My dad and his brother Cicero, played for dances up at the old Ash Creek schoolhouse about once a month, for a good many years. That was about thirty-five or forty miles from where we lived. I remember one time we decided to go on up to the mountains to Turkey Creek, in the Chiricahuas, about fifteen miles up the road from there, and have a picnic before the dance. By the time we got home the next day a little after sunrise, Daddy had changed seven flat tires. He always had his tire tools and patches with him. We didn't have the best tires in the country.

Since we lived out in the country, and our closest neighbor lived close to a mile away, we had a lot of room to roam. I was several years younger than my older brothers, but had three sisters that were nearer to my age. We ran wild like a bunch of jack rabbits. One time we were down by Whitewater Creek, (we called it "the big river") and it was flooding real high. We were getting thirsty, and it kind of looked like that was the only water available. We were a mile or more from home, so my sister, Agnes, one year younger than I, decided to get a drink from the river. I was too scared of the flooded river, so went a couple hundred feet up a little side gully and found a mud puddle to drink out of. When I got back to where the girls were, my older sister, Marjorie, had just dragged Agnes out of the river where she had almost drowned. We never told anybody about that incident for many years.

We also had a lot of fun playing in Old Man Oliver's haystacks, which were about a half a mile north of our place. He stacked his Johnson grass hay in loose stacks, and we liked to climb up and slide down the sides. We would also dig short tunnels into the stacks. I'm sure the old feller didn't appreciate what we did, but I don't think he ever caught us or bothered us.

I guess it's natural for little kids to want to fly. We used to go up on top of our chicken house with a big piece of cardboard, and jump off, but none of us ever glided very far.

When I was about five or six years old, I guess you could say I started chasing rainbows. Our Grandma Stoner lived about a quarter mile up the road from us, and liked to collect arrowheads and other artifacts. She would give us hard candy for the arrowheads we found. That was the only candy we ever got, except maybe once a year at Christmas. We spent a lot of time hunting arrowheads, and I still hunt them every chance I get.

I well remember the first real money I ever made. I must have been five or six years old at the time. I worked my heart out for about half a day, picking cotton for old man Porter over at Double Adobe. I picked ten pounds of cotton at two cents a pound, and got two big dimes for my work. When lunch time came, we all went in the house to eat. When I was about halfway through with my meal, the Old man Porter told me I would have to give him one of my dimes to pay for my meal. I ran out of that house so fast I almost knocked the door down, and never looked back. I knew where my folks were working on a house about a mile cross country from there, and I made a bee-line to where they were. I most likely ran most of the way just in case they might follow me. I had never seen that much money in my life, and nobody was going to get it away from me. I don't think I ever went back to Porter's again. I'm sure they were kidding me, but I never took a chance.

We, as a family, spent several seasons in the Double Adobe area, helping to harvest vegetables, as there were several small truck farms in the area. We all made what little spending money we had doing this. For about ten years we helped Frank Murphy harvest his onions. One year he had a lot of silver dollars that he paid us with. Later that fall, when we were getting wood for our heating and cook stove, we found a wooden box not too far from his house, with coin imprints in it.

It seems there was a post office robbery about thirty years before this and there were four people involved. Three of the outlaws were caught, and the fourth was never apprehended. We just figured Murphy was the fourth man, cause the other three had lived in the same area. A few years later, another kid and I found where one of the other caches had been dug up. I found one 1903 Indian head penny, and a 1909 Lincoln head penny. This was about the time the other outlaws were released from prison.

When I was in the third grade, I was privileged to go on a trip to the mountains with my older brothers, Charlie and Clifford. We ended up in Red Rock Canyon (the canyon South of Rucker Canyon, a well known recreation area). We messed around up there all day, and when we got ready to come home, the car wouldn't start. It was kinda stormy, so we decided to walk out to an old deserted homestead about five or six miles down the canyon. There was an old dugout cellar there we planned to use for shelter for the night. We walked til it seemed like out tongues would drag the ground and it got too dark to see anything. Finally, we decided to stop for the night. My brothers built a lean-to out of tree branches, and we spent a pretty miserable night, cause it rained a little off and on. The next morning at sunrise, we got up and looked around, and the cellar we were headed for was about a hundred feet from where we had spent the night. After we thawed out a little, we went down in the orchard that was there, and filled up on the apples and pears that were ripe in the trees there. That was the best fruit I ever ate. I guess because we hadn't eaten much the day before. We walked back up to the car that morning, and Charlie figured out how to get it going. On the way home, we were hitting the high spots in that old stripped down Model-A, when a big calf ran out in the road. We ran over him with both wheels, and scorched him with the exhaust pipe, but he got up and ran away. I sure had a good story to tell at "show and tell" that week at school.

We always enjoyed sitting around the house, listening to Daddy tell stories about things that he saw and did when he was young. One story, in particular comes to mind. I wish we had had some way to record a lot of his stories, but we didn't.

In the story I have in mind, (Daddy was about ten or twelve years old at the time) he and his daddy had taken a load of turkeys to Bowie to sell. They were on their way home, when a Mexican climbed up on the back of the wagon with a big knife in his hand, ready to do business. I guess my dad saw him coming and gave warning. I guess Grandpa always had a loaded 44-40 rifle beside him in the wagon, and wasn't afraid to use it in self-defense. Daddy said Grandpa just eared back the hammer of that old rifle and shot that Mexican dead on the spot. He just dragged him over behind some bushes, and threw a few rocks and brush on him, and they went on home and never looked back. Grandpa told Daddy not to tell anyone about it, and he probably never did, until his Daddy was dead and gone. That was one Mexican that made the mistake of bringing a knife to a gunfight.

Another story happened several years later when Daddy was working for a dairy farm, peddling milk, up in Ray, Arizona. It seems like he was pouring milk into a bottle on some feller's doorstep, and talking to the feller, when an ex-deputy sheriff stepped around the corner of the house, and shot this feller right through the cheeks. I guess it took out a few teeth, but didn't hurt the guy too much. He never said what happened to the shooter.

Later on, in Douglas, Arizona, he got into a shooting scrape of his own. He was peddling milk this time, also. He never gave too many details to the story, but I guess a storekeeper on his route where he had been selling milk, thought Daddy was a little too friendly to his wife. One day when Daddy stopped there on his milk route, this feller came out of the store with a rifle in his hand and threatened to kill Daddy. Daddy happened to have his own rifle in the car and didn't want to die without a fight. He reached up behind the seat of his Model-A roadster, and got his rifle out. The gun was a model 95-30-40 Winchester. When he levered a shell into the chamber, the gun went off, and the bullet went real close to the old store-man's head. The man died a few days later, possibly from the concussion. Daddy spent the night in jail for disturbing the peace, and went back to peddling milk the next day. He never did say if the old man's concerns were justified or not. Knowing Daddy, they could have been.

Daddy was quite a story teller, and had a lot of good stories to tell. Momma was a little more laid back and the stories she had to tell were not quite as exciting as Daddy's. She was about the hardest working person I never knew, though. After all of us kids were out of diapers, she worked side by side with Daddy, building houses all over the Sulphur Springs Valley. The older kids were able to look after the younger ones by then.

During World War II, Daddy worked over at Fort Huachuca, and was gone all week and came home on weekends. He usually came home in a good mood, but once in a while he would tangle with old Joe Barlycorn before he came home. He was half Irish, and half Indian, and sometimes "old Joe" would make him kinda mean. Whenever he showed up in this shape, we would all scatter like a bunch of quail til he sobered up a little. One time he picked up a bicycle wheel and threw it, and hit my brother, Clifford, in the head with it. It didn't hurt Clifford too bad, but it sobered the 'old man' up pretty fast. "That was the only time he ever came close to hurting any of us. He very seldom ever even spanked any of us, but if we did something that we shouldn't have, he had a way of talking to us that was worse than a whipping. All and all, Momma and Daddy both had a lot of patience with all of us.

Sometime in the fall or winter of 1946, I had my first and only run-in with alcohol. We were up the road about a mile at the neighbor's. The adults were having a card party, and we kids were running around outside. There happened to be a washtub full of beer on ice out there. I thought I should try it out, since the old folks thought it was so good. I slipped out and drank a couple bottles of the nasty stuff while nobody was looking. Before the night was over, I was pretty sick, and had a toothache to boot. I must have passed out before we got home, because I woke up in the car the next morning. I learned my lesson faster than some people in this country, and have never taken a drink of alcohol since. I sometimes wish some of the other things I have tried over the years would have worked out as well.

I started to school in 1946, also. I was fortunate to be able to spend my first grade at the little country Frontier School. We were kinda like one big happy family. There were three three girls, and three boys, counting myself, in my first grade class. The girls were Barbara Dale, her cousin, Julia Pursley, and another girl, named Sandy Collier.

The other two boys were Billy White and Gary Heise. We all had good times playing games, like Wolf over the river, and others that I can't remember. All eight grades would get involved in our games. That year was the last year that they had a school at Frontier. The county decided that the valley kids should be bused to Bisbee to school. I was never very happy in school after that. My two friends, Billy and Gary moved away, and I never saw either one of them again. The two cousins, Barbara and Julia, stayed in the area, and we went to school together til I quit school in my junior year of high school. I still see them once in a while at reunions. The other girl, Sandy, moved away also, and I've never seen her since, either.

After we had to give up our little school on Frontier Road, we went to school at Greenway school for a year. I don't remember having too much fun that year, at all. I can only remember the name of one person that went to school there in my class. I only remember him because he kinda bullied me around all year. He never did hurt me physically, but he was never very nice. He was Eddie Sharpe, and I think his daddy was deputy sheriff in the county. I never saw him again til we started high school together. He kinda apologized for the misery he had caused me, and we got along well in high school.

In 1948, we started school over at Lowell School, and things were a little better over there. There were more poor kids there, and the valley kids were not looked down on so bad. That was the year that the McDonald twins, Pat and Mike, started to school. They were a couple years behind me, but we got along pretty good. They both had a slight speech impediment, and their teacher would sometimes get me out of my classroom to interpret for them. I was the only one that could understand them sometimes. We had a lot of good times together over the years, and I still hear from Pat once in a while, after close to sixty years of friendship. Pat and Mike and I ran around a lot together, over the years, and had lots of adventures. One time we decided we would try to find an old Indian campground their dad had located sometime before. He had told them where it was, so we thought we could find it. We headed out down the old railroad grade, that ran by their house, to see if we could find some artifacts. We got about five miles down (actually, it was up the valley) and finally found the place. We were getting pretty hungry and thirsty by this time, so I got the wise idea that we should walk on up to Grizzel's orchard, and borrow a few peaches to keep us going. It was only five or six miles farther up the valley. We were really hungry and thirsty by the time we got there. We slipped in the lower end of the orchard, and hadn't even got our bellies full yet, when this feller came tearing around the corner in a Jeep. I could see right away he had a big shotgun in his hand and would likely fill our asses with lead if we ran. So I held the twins back til he got where we were at. I kinda explained the situation, and he let us go on our way. He said he thought we were trying to steal his watermelons. Anyhow, we still had about ten or fifteen miles to walk back to McDonald's house. We decided to go back by way of Elfrida, as we had a chance to catch a ride out on the highway. We did finally catch a ride, but I'm sure we walked twenty or twenty-five miles that day. I'm sure we slept good that night and we never duplicated the trip. Many years later, my sister, Marjorie and her grandkids did locate the place we were looking for, but the University of Arizona had taken most of the good stuff already. I've been there a time or two in recent years, and still find a few arrowheads.

The twins daddy died in the early 1950's and they moved to Oregon. So I found other kids to pal around with.

Larry Fowler and his nephew, Wayne Lovett, were two boys that I palled around with when we went to Lowell School together. I would stay in town sometimes, and they would stay out at our place sometimes. When I stayed in town, we would prowl around in some of the old mines up by Bisbee. We rolled a mine car or two off the hill for excitement, and a few other innocent pranks. The one I remember best was the time we stole the chicken. If I remember right, we actually skipped the afternoon classes of school to have our chicken Bar-B-Q. There were several chicken pens just a few hundred yards down the creek from the school. We slipped into one of these pens, and grabbed the first chicken we could get our hands on. I don't know how we kept from getting caught, 'cause it was the middle of the day. Anyhow, we took this chicken down the creek a ways and tried to butcher the old thing. I don't think we ever did get it killed, and I know we never butchered or cooked it. It happened to be an old setting hen, and I don't believe there was over two ounces of meat on the whole thing. I guess you know that was the first, last, and only chicken I ever had a hand in stealing.

I never saw either of those boys much after I quit school in 1957, but I did speak to Larry on the phone, not too long before he was shot dead by a taxi driver in Anchorage, Alaska, about seven or eight years ago. I don't know what ever happened to Wayne Lovett. (He died five or six years ago).

Along in early 1953, when my older brother, Charlie, was working on a farm not far from Willcox at Kansas Settlement, a black man and another young feller went in a little store up there and killed the widow-woman that owned and operated the place. I guess they took all the money they could find, and then tried to burn up the evidence. I guess it didn't take the sheriff's department long to figure out who did the job. I heard at the time that the cowboys who caught the older feller roped and dragged him for a distance. They were thinking about hanging him, I guess, but they couldn't find a tall enough tree, or possibly cooler heads prevailed, and he lived to stand trial. I understand that he was executed legally several years later. I'm not sure what happened to his accomplice.

For several years after this incident, there was a road sign on each end of Willcox stating "BLACK MAN, DON'T LET THE SUN SET ON YOU IN WILLCOX" (That was before political correctness.)

Along about this time or a year or so before, an old friend of my Dad's was railroaded out of the country by his own kin-folks, on a trumped-up cattle rustling charge.

Old Bill Price had a nice ranch close to Turkey Creek, in the Chiricahua Mountains. He had also found a pretty large treasure not too long prior to this. His greedy kin-folks thought they could find this money and dig it up if he was in prison. I guess the plot kinda backfired.

I guess that when Bill was in county jail, waiting for his trial, he talked the county sheriff into taking him out to the ranch to dig his money up. His kin had already been there and dug several holes in his yard, but hadn't found the treasure. He went ahead and dug up the money to live on while he was in exile in Texas. (They sentenced him to ten years out of the state of Arizona) He came back after ten years and lived his life out on his ranch, as near as I know.

When I started school at Bisbee High it was customary for the freshman boys to give the "B" a new coat of white-wash every year before the big "Turkey Day" football game. This was always played against Douglas to decide who would retain the Copper Pick for that year.

When the day came to do this job, we all gathered at the trail-head to the "B". A group of upper class-men, called the "Drillers", were assigned to keep us all lined out.

I grabbed a water bucket, filled it with water and headed up the hill with fifty or sixty other boys doing similar jobs. When we got up there we mixed some lime and water and started spreading it around the "B". things were going pretty good til I felt the first few drops of sweat. About that time I had a change of plans.

I grabbed a bucket and one of my good buddies and headed down the trail. I can't remember who it was that went down there with me, but I know as soon as we got out of sight of any drillers we made a mad dash to the best thicket we could find. We had us a nice siesta for three or four hours while them other fifty or sixty boys did a bang-up job of painting the "B". When we thought the job was nearly done we went down and got one more load of water and were done for the day. All-in-all it was a good day.

A couple years later I was honored to be a driller myself, and kinda wondered how many freshmen pulled the same trick we did.

We (as Drillers) also had the job of lighting the "B" on fire on Thanksgiving night. We carried tons of old greasy rags up there and outlined the "B" with them and set them on fire. I don't know if they do that anymore or not, but it was a pretty sight to see. Those were some of my good times at Bisbee High School.

The Mauzy boys were two other boys I ran around with some, after I got in high school. Lloyd and Gene happened to have an old Model-A Ford roadster that they would drive down to our house on weekends sometimes. We would run all over the valley, and have a lot of fun in that old car. One day we were on our way home from the mountains, and we hit a bump in the road a little too hard. That old Ford started making a horrible noise, so we limped on in to our house and parked it. The boys rode the school bus to school the next day, and asked my daddy if he could try to fix their car for them.

Daddy took the oil pan off the old thing the next day, and found that a splash pan in there had broke loose and was hitting the piston rods. He threw the splash pan away, and the car was good as new. He made up a bill for the boys to give to their Dad. He had a list as long as your arm, including six spark plugs. Seems like the bill came to a pretty good sum when he included twenty-five cents for labor. Old Tom Mauzy, the boys dad, who was an owner of Bledsoe, Mauzy Motors, was a little more serious minded than Daddy was, and I guess he hit the ceiling when the boys showed him the statement. They said it took them a while to convince him it was only a joke. Daddy wouldn't take a nickel for helping our friends like that.

Gene went in the army not too long after this incident, and I didn't see him again for about thirty years. About six months before my Dad died in 1986, Daddy was in the hospital in Tucson. My younger sister, Violet, happened to be working with Gene's wife at the time. He learned I was down there from Oregon to see Daddy. So we decided to get together in Daddie's hospital room. We had a nice visit, and a good laugh over the incident I just described. That was the last time I saw Gene, and almost the last time I saw Daddy. I visited Daddy once or twice after that, and had to come back to Oregon to work. He died on December 5, 1986, before I was ever able to see him again. As for Gene, I learned that he had committed suicide not too long after our visit. It seems that Old Joe Barleycorn had too big a holt on him and he couldn't take it any longer. At least that's what his brother, Lloyd told me not long after it happened.

As for Lloyd, he and I had another adventure in that old Model-A that's worth telling about. When school let out in 1956, he and I decided we wanted to play cowboy. His Dad was good friends with Joe Kitchen, who was the general superintendent of the Diamond-A Ranches in New Mexico, and the Boquillas Ranch in Arizona, some of the biggest ranches around.

A few days after school let out, we got out bedrolls together, and hit the trail for New Mexico. Our first stop was over at the Gray Ranch, South of Animas about fifteen miles. They didn't need any help, so we went across the valley to the Hatchet Ranch.

We got there in time to have lunch with the crew. They didn't need any help, either. After we had eaten, we were in the yard, and I heard a real loud scream. There had been a little dwarf girl there when we ate, and I thought something had happened to her, so I ran over to see if I could help. The only thing I found was a peacock rooster, screaming his head off. I had never heard one before, so it kinda scared me.

After we left the Hatchet Ranch, we headed on toward Deming, where Joe Kitchen's office was. It got dark on us before we got there, so we pulled the old Model-A out in the brush to spend the night. We rolled out our bedrolls on the ground, and crawled down in them for the night. In a minute or two we heard a coyote howl real close by. Another answered from another direction, and a couple more called from the other two sides. We were surrounded!

A short time before this, there had been a bad rabies scare close to where I lived in the valley. Two or three people had been bitten by rabid animals. This was fresh in my mind, so it really added to the fear that we felt.

Anyhow, we laid there in them bedrolls for close on to thirty seconds, and got up and spent the rest of the night sitting up in the front seat of that old Model-A Ford coupe. I don't think we slept very much, but at least we didn't get ate up by them hydrophobied coyotes.

We found Joe Kitchen's office the next morning, and he sent us up to Engle, which is about eighteen miles East of Truth or Consequences. Lloyd was able to go to work the next day. I was still too young to work, 'cause you had to be sixteen, and I lacked a few months of being that old. But I figured out a remedy for that problem right quick. I had my sixteenth birthday four months early that year. My Social Security card still has June 13, instead of October 13, 1940, as my birth date.

We had a real enjoyable month and a half that year. We worked through the spring roundup. It was the first year the ranch had quit using a chuck wagon. We stayed at the cow camps at night, instead.

They gave Lloyd a string of horses to ride while we were there, but I just worked as a ground man. My main job was to flank and hold the calves while they were being branded. We worked in pairs, one on the head, and the other held their hind legs, while they were being branded, getting shots, and being de-horned.

We would get up before daylight and get ready for the day. The wrangler would bring in the horses and put them in the corral, or if there wasn't a corral handy, we would use a rope corral. That was a corral made by the cowboys standing in a big circle with their lass-ropes stretched between them. Each cowboy would call out the name of the horse he was going to ride that day, and the wagon boss would rope that horse for him. He used what they called a "hoolian" loop to catch each animal. In this type of roping you only swing the rope one time, and it don't get the horses all excited.

We, or the cowboys, would ride in a big circle and gather all the cows and calves they could find and bring them to a central area, where the corral was located, for branding. We would brand what they brought in, and the rest of the day was ours to do as we pleased. We were usually done by two or three o'clock. Sometimes we would drive the A-Model to town and cruise the streets, but lots of times we'd just laze around the camps. Lloyd got bucked off and broke his arm not too long after we got there. He was kinda on light duty after that. All in all, it was a very enjoyable experience. I stayed in touch with one family I met that summer, for about forty years. My wife and I exchanged Christmas cards with Leo and Lana Turner until they both died of old age, not too many years ago. We visited with them in person many times through the years, also.

Another set of friends I ran around with some, was the Dodson kids from Elfrida. Their dad was the ginner at the cotton gin where my brother, Charlie, and my Daddy worked. I would ride up there with Charlie or Daddy and spend the weekend sometimes.

The boys names were James, Lynn, and Shot. Shot was about my age, and we had some fun times together. We liked to torment the yard-man, (the guy that hauled the bales of cotton out in the storage yard.) We would sometimes spray him with the pyrene fire extinguisher, and run like the wind, so he wouldn't catch us. We also spent a little time requisitioning gasoline for my old 1932 Plymouth jalopy. We had an Okie credit card, and some of the trucks loaded with cotton had to spend the night there. They had more fuel than they needed, so we would try to lighten their load. We just took a little bit from each truck, so it wouldn't be noticed, but I'm sure some of them farmers weren't fooled. We never got caught, anyhow. However, we thought we were caught one time. There were several of us involved this time. There was the three Dodson boys, Gene Fowler, Clifford (my next older brother) and myself.

There was a well rig set up about a half mile from where we lived, and we knew there was a fifty gallon barrel of gas sitting there, just waiting to be tapped. So along about dark one night, we jumped in one of our old jalopies and went down to see what we could do about it.

We got down there and got the lid off the barrel, and just got the siphon hose running good, when a set of car lights showed up about fifty yards from where we were standing. You never saw a bunch of boys scatter so fast in your life. I took about two steps and a hand grabbed me by the collar. It happened to be Gene Fowler, the cool one of the bunch. He just said "hold your ground, we'll talk our way out of this." That's the way Gene was.

In about ten seconds we heard some awful screeching sounds, and I knew the Dodson boys had found the barb-wire fence that was about a hundred feet out there. I don't know how much damage it did to the fence, but when the boys showed back up later, they were skinned up pretty bad. I think Clifford knew the fence was there so he came out all right.

Anyhow, when the smoke and dust cleared, and brother Charlie got out of his car, laughing his guts out, we called the boys in and had a good laugh ourselves.

Seems like Charlie had word somewhere that the county sheriff was kinda keeping an eye on that well rig, and he didn't want us to get caught. I don't think we ever bothered that rig again.

Another time Shot and I had a fun time, was a hunting trip. It seems like someone had seen a bear up in John Long Canyon, and we were always wanting to get us a bear. John Long Canyon is the next canyon North of Rucker Canyon, and about forty or fifty miles by road from our house in the valley.

We gathered up a big crew, this time including the Dodson boys and their dad, "Tiny" (300 Lbs.), and my brother, Clifford. That was a pretty good carload. We took Tiny's car, which was a fairly new Chevy.

We got up there and made a pretty good hunt without any luck. When we got back to the car, we had two flat tires. Since there was only one spare, and we didn't have any tire tools, somebody had to go for help. Shot and I were designated to go for help.

We struck out in the late morning, and took what we thought was the shortest road out of there. We thought we might catch a ride, sooner or later. As it turned out, it was later. We walked for about ten hours, and close to thirty miles before we caught a ride. We were about ten miles from home when Ralph "Mutt" Morrow, the local game warden, saw us coming down the road with our tongues dragging the ground, and took pity on us. He was going the other direction, but turned around and took us back to the house. He pumped us pretty hard to find out just where we broke down, but didn't get much information. I'm sure he knew we were poaching, but he never pushed it too hard.

When he let us off, my Daddy asked him in for supper. He refused, saying he saw some dove hunters down the road he wanted to check out. He was gone about five minutes, and was talking to the dove hunters about two hundred yards down the road, when Ed McDonald (the twin's Dad) drove up in the ranch jeep. He reached in the back of the jeep, and threw a half a deer, he had poached, over his shoulder and brought it in the house. This was almost the only time that he brought us meat like that, and the closest either one of our families ever came to getting caught.

Soon as we could get the tire tools and patches together, we jumped in my old '32 Plymouth, and went back up and got the rest of the crew.

I haven't heard from any of the Dodsons since they left the area not too long after that. But Shot showed up down home a few years ago, and said he was working at Mercury, Nevada. If he's still alive, I'm sure he remembers our little excursion.

Another set of our friends was Dickie and Danny Neilson. They lived up in Bisbee. We got acquainted in high school. We would spend our lunch hour, from school, down at the five and dime soda fountain. I had a part-time job on weekends, sorting onions for Frank Murphy, who I mentioned before, and was able to buy us each a soda every day.

One day we got down there in the alley behind the drug store, and you could see blood stains on the street. Seems like some feller got upset with his business partners the night before, and shot and killed both of them. I guess one of them had died inside the building, and the other had died out in that alley. They tried their best to clean up the blood, but it showed up for quite a while after that. I think the killer got a two or three year sentence for the killings, 'cause Cochise County was pretty easy on criminals at that time.

We had a little trip that I thought was worth mentioning, also.

We decided we wanted to make a trip up to the Chiricahua Mountains for the weekend. We let the folks know about where we would be, in case we had problems. We climbed in an old stripped down 1941 Ford that we had, and headed out. We got up into upper Pine Canyon, which is about sixty miles from home, and spent a couple days running up and down the canyon in that old car. I think we killed a squirrel or two and ate them for supper. We never tried to get any big game, 'cause it was too far from home and too risky. When it came time to head for home, we checked our gas, and found that we didn't have any. We had a pretty good camp, and still had a few groceries left. So we decided to spend an extra night. We figured my folks knew where we were, and would come looking for us in a few days.

I guess the Neilson boys parents and kinfolks were not quite as understanding as mine. They had the law and everybody else looking for us. I guess their cousin, Gay Hill (who I was sweet on at the time) and her Momma even had a big cry over their lost cousins and boyfriend. Anyhow, that's what they said when we got back.

About ten or eleven o'clock Monday morning, we heard a car coming down the canyon. Sure enough, it was old Charlie, and he had a can of gas to pour into old tin lizzy, and we were on our way home. All and all, it was a fun trip.

I never saw the Neilson boys after I quit school, until seven or eight years ago, at the funeral of our good friend, Don Gray. Don had married Gay Hill not too long after our trip to the Chiricahuas. Don and Gay and I stayed friends all those years.

Along in the late forty's and early fifty's, A quite a few families were moving out of our area. It was a pretty tough country to make a go of it. There were a quite a few deserted houses around the area within walking distance. (five or six miles.) We kids liked to go and explore these deserted places, 'cause sometimes people would leave good stuff behind. Most anything usable was good stuff to us.

Anyhow, old Charlie came home with a nice pocket knife one day, and it didn't take the rest of us too long to find where it came from. Seems like Grandma Turman, and her grandson, Jiggs Gibbons, were in the process of moving to California, and their house had been vacant for several weeks. Charlie had found a way to get in the house, and had nabbed a good knife.

The rest of us decided we should get in on the goodies, so we made a trip or two up there and got ourselves a few trinkets. I think I got a pocket knife, and a couple of my sisters got a little stuff they liked, nothing to amount to much.

One day Clifford and I, and I think it was Gene Fowler, I can't remember for sure, (not long before Charlie died, I accused him, and he didn't remember anything about it, so it must have been Gene.) Anyhow, I know there were three of us, and we decided to make another run on that deserted house. We hadn't got started to scrounging real good when we happened to look out the window of that old house. We saw an old Model A touring car drive up in the yard. It was too late to run, so we all three dived under the nearest bed 'til the storm passed

It was Grandma Turman, and Jiggs, coming back to move the rest of their belongings. They came in the house and stood right beside the bed we were under, and discussed whether to start loading stuff right away, or to wait 'til the next day. Grandma even started to get her broom and start cleaning, but decided against it. They only stayed for ten or fifteen minutes, but that's a long time when you're holding your breath. If any of us had eaten pinto beans that day, or had a cold, we would have probably ended up in front of a judge. But we managed to get by without getting caught. When they finally left, it didn't take us too long to get out of there. And we made sure they were gone for good before we ever went back.

That was the last time I saw Jiggs Gibbons feet for about fifty or sixty years. He still lives in California, and he came through the country down there when Charlie was on his death bed. We had a nice visit, but you can bet I never told him "the rest of the story"

We also had a quite a lot of fun going to old deserted mines up in the mountains. Once in a while, we would find a case of dynamite setting around them old mine tunnels. In order to keep someone from getting hurt by it, we would load it up and take it home where it would be safe. We would also take any fuse and blasting caps, 'cause they can be dangerous, too, in the wrong hands.

One day we went up to Middle March, (about ten miles west of Pearce, in the Dragoon Mountains) which is about sixty miles from where we lived. We were in Charlie's Model A roadster, if I remember right. We got up there and found a full case of dynamite in an old mine tunnel, that some careless prospector had abandoned, probably at least twenty four hours before we got there. There was also a nice roll of fuse, and a nearly full can of blasting caps. We couldn't leave anything that dangerous laying around, so we loaded it up in the rumble seat compartment of that old Ford, and hauled it home with us. I sat on that case of powder all the way home, 'cause I knew it was safe. The blasting caps were up in the front with the older boys.

Anyhow, we made it home with our cargo, and had a bang-up good time for several weeks. We blew up a lot of stuff, but I think the only real damage we did was to Daddy's cement water tank.

The families of the community got together on week-ends at the time. We played baseball on some vacant property up the road about a quarter mile from our house. One day while we were up there playing ball, I happened to look down toward the house, and saw a big geyser go up in the air down there. A few seconds later I heard the explosion. It didn't take me too long to get down there, 'cause I didn't want to miss out on the fun. It was Clifford, and we set off a few more charges before Daddy showed up and told us he thought that dynamite might be hard on his pond. We didn't see how it could hurt it because the water went so high. We found out the next morning that the Old Man was right. The pond was empty as my head. We got some cement and tried to patch it, but it never did hold water very good after that.

Another time, we were getting a little low on fresh venison, so we headed up to Abbot Canyon, which was our favorite poaching area. We had a little (eight or ten sticks) of dynamite left over from our last heist, and thought it would be fun to see how many big rocks we could roll off the hills with it. We were almost up to the mountains, which were about ten miles from home, when we ran out of gas. We had hit a rock, and put a hole in the gas tank. We knew we were on our own, so we struck out walking for home.

My Grandma Stoner had died a few years before that, and my folks had used her vacant house for community get-togethers. This particular night they were having a card party and a dance combined, I think. They were getting wound up pretty good by the time we got back from the mountains.

We thought we could liven up the party a bit by setting a small charge out in the field about a hundred yards from the house. Actually, it seemed to have the opposite affect. Nobody knew we were within a hundred miles ('cause we were supposed to be in the mountains.)so they didn't see too much humor in it when them four sticks of powder went off. I can't remember for sure if we ever showed our little pin-heads, but I do remember a quite a few tail-lights heading up the road. That was the end of the party, for sure. I think the boys involved in this little escapade were Clifford, Gene and Larry Fowler, and myself, but I can't remember for sure. I know we had a lot of fun.

Some of the best times we had as a family were during the regular deer hunting season. Hunting season always opened on Friday, for some reason. As soon as we got home from school on Thursday. We would load up and head out to our favorite hunting site, in what Daddy called Shaw's canyon. Actually, it was the lower end of Pine Canyon, but when Daddy lived about a mile from there, as a kid, a family by the name of Shaw had lived there. When we got there, we would set up a quick camp with a big bonfire and all the good stuff. The smell of that old oak wood burning is something I'll never forget. We would sleep out under the stars, and crawl out before daybreak to start our hunt.

When we scattered out to start our hunt, Daddy always said "If you hear a shot, put on the skillet and we'll have heart and liver for lunch." His predictions usually came true, 'cause he was a pretty good shot, and knew where the deer were going to be. We usually filled our tags on the first week-end of the season, but not always.

One season (I think it was the second year I had my license) we hadn't filled up our tags up in the Chiricahuas, so we hunted the second week-end in the Swisshelm Mountains. There were mostly white-tail deer up in Shaw's Canyon, but there were some nice mule deer in the Swisshelms. Along about sundown on the last day of season, I heard some shots where I knew Momma should be. I hightailed it over, and found her chasing a big mule deer buck that she had broken both hind legs on. I happened to get to him before she did, and finished him off with a shot to the head. He was a nice trophy four-point mule deer. Somehow, we scraped up the money to have the head mounted. The head is still hanging on the living room wall in the folks old home-place, more than fifty years later.

Another hunting trip I remember was a year or two later. Three of the Fowler boys were with us on this trip; Larry, Gene, and their older brother, Bill. We were hunting over the hill from Shaw's Canyon, in what we called Five Mile Canyon. Along late in the morning, I heard some shots a half a mile or so away. I knew our party was probably the only ones in the area, so I headed that way, to see if I could help with the butchering. I hadn't gone too far when I heard Bill Fowler hollering. When I got to him, his hair was standing on end, and he looked pretty scared. He said he had shot a big bear, and needed some help to get it out. About that time, Gene showed up to see what he had. Sure enough, there was a big black bear laying up in a manzanita thicket, dead. He had a big manzanita limb clamped in his teeth, and was dead as a mackerel. Poor old Bill was still shaking pretty bad, and Gene didn't show any signs that he wanted to gut the thing, so I grabbed my trusty old pocket knife, and got the job done for them. Then we went and got the old "41" Ford strip-down, and a little more help. It took four of us to pack that bear off that hill. We didn't want to ruin his hide, so we tied him upside down on a long pole. That's about the hardest way I ever saw to pack anything, but we got him out. We loaded him in that old Ford and took him to camp.

We still had a couple days to hunt, so we went on hunting, and failed to skin the bear out like we should have. By the time we got it skinned out, the meat was spoiled, but Bill had a nice bearskin rug. Bill and Larry are both gone now, and the last I heard Gene was living in Tucson, after a long career of mining gold up in the Yukon Territory of Canada. I called him and asked him for a job not too long before Larry got killed, but he said he couldn't hire anybody but Canadians.

Another trip I remember didn't produce any venison or bear meat, but did almost produce something more valuable; a small piece of history. In order to explain this statement, I have to go back to one of Daddy's stories of long-ago.

It seems like sometime back in the 1920's, or possibly earlier, his brother, Cicero Kennedy (we called him Uncle Cy) was working in a mining camp up in the Swisshelm Mountains. The name of the mine was the Heffner Mine. It seems like they had a camp cook that wasn't quite ready for "Chef of the year awards". I guess they tolerated the old feller for quite a while, but he didn't seem to improve too much. Mining in the underground mines, tends to make people hungry and a little cranky. One day, I guess this old boy from Texas got about all he could take of these less than gourmet meals. He pulled his six-shooter and shot the coffee pot off the stove. I guess it didn't take that cook too long to get out of there after that.

Well, about thirty or forty years later, I happened to be hunting up by the old deserted Heffner Mine, when I thought about this story. I wandered around the old mine for a while to figure out the lay of the land. I hadn't been there long when, sure enough, I found that old coffee pot with the bullet holes in it. Instead of taking the thing with me, I put it up in a mesquite bush and left it there. I never had any occasion to go back up there for another forty years or more. A few years back I made a special trip up there to see if I could find that pot, but could never locate it. It would have been a nice keep-sake and conversation piece.

Along toward the end of the school year of 1956-1957, I had a run-in with one of my teachers, and it kinda soured me on school. Old Lady Shreve (junior English teacher) gave us an assignment that I was not able to complete. We had to write a theme and typewrite it. I didn't know how to typewrite, and wasn't going to impose on anyone to do it for me, so I handed in an unfinished theme, written in ink.

I was able to keep about a 90% average grade on the rest of my work, but when I got my report card, she failed me. I still had several weeks of school, but I knew I was doomed, so I quit handing in my work. She called me on it one day, and I informed her that I wasn't getting paid for my work, so I wasn't doing it. She sent me to study hall and I never looked back.

Since I knew I was not likely to return to good old Bisbee High School, I decided a few days before school let out, to give them a going-away present.

My brother, Clifford, and Bobby McDonald had a bunch of coon dogs they were trying to train. They used skunk musk in a bottle to teach them not to chase skunks. I just borrowed a little bit of this training fluid, and spread it around the halls of B.H.S. A few people knew who did it, and after that I was known as "the skunk of Bisbee High".

That was the end of my academic achievement, although I did get a G.E.D. Certificate when I was living in Mitchell, Oregon, thirteen years later. (I've never had occasion to use it.)

That summer I never did get a good enough job to buy my school clothes, so I started my career in the school of hard knocks. Murphy had quit raising onions, and that had always been our mainstay.

School of hard knocks 1957-2006

That fall I had another premature birthday, only this time it was a whole year early. The cotton gin up at Elfrida required that you be eighteen to go to work there, but didn't check it too close. They didn't have computers and such in them days.

A few days after my seventeenth birthday, I hired on at the gin. My job was to dress the press. There was a turntable with two chambers, and while one was filling with cotton, I would get the other chamber ready for the next bale. It was a pretty monotonous job, and we worked twelve hours, seven days a week. It kept me out of mischief and was the biggest money I had made at the time. I was getting a whole dollar an hour. I made enough to buy me a usable car and had money left over. I worked there for about two and a half months, til the cotton harvest was over, then went on to bigger and better things.

Sometime early in 1958, I went to work at a little sawmill up in Willcox, about sixty miles from home. I stayed with a good friend of mine and his wife (Buddy and Audrie Garcia) We had been friends since I started to school at Frontier. He was a year older than I was.

I worked at that sawmill for a couple months. I would go home on weekends, and back to Willcox on Monday morning. Sometimes I would be a little late getting back on Monday morning. This happened a couple times, and about the third time, there was a big black man working in my place, so I had to move on. The last check I got from them bounced, and I don't think I ever did get paid for my last week of work.

I had picked up three hobos on my way home the week before, and thinking I had a good job, I had given them almost the last five dollars I had, to keep them going til they could go to work on a lettuce farm out at Kansas Settlement. I never saw them again, but never regretted helping them.

When I lost my job at Willcox, I decided to go over to Engle, New Mexico, and try to go to work on the ranch again. They didn't need anybody, but I was able to get a part-time job in Truth or Consequences.

Lou and Rachael McDonald (the estranged wife and daughter of Burlie McDonald, who was the wagon boss for the ranch in 1956) gave me a place to stay, and got me a job cleaning stables for a doctor who also had race horses. I worked there for a little more than a week, but wasn't able to do the job to suit the old feller, so I had to move on.

I had often wondered what Colorado looked like, so I headed North. I seems like I spent a little time in Pagosa Springs, when I first got to Colorado. Hudspeth had just opened a new sawmill there, but they weren't operating yet. I didn't stay around there but a few hours, and went on to Durango and points beyond. I got almost to the top of Molas Lake Pass, between Durango and Silverton, and my car with the bald tires, spun out. Some nice feller in a Jeep pickup pulled me out of the ditch, and headed me back down the hill to Durango.

I drove around the Durango area for a day or two, looking for work. Finally, a highway patrolman noticed my expired license plate, and took me down to the police station. I sat in the police station for several hours, playing my Baby Gibson guitar, while they decided what to do with me. They thought the car might have been stolen, but learned different after a few hours. They did, however, impound my car til I could get license on it. I didn't have any place to stay, cause I was living in my car, so they gave me a bed, and a morning meal at the jailhouse in the drunk-tank.

The next morning I located an old deserted house on the edge of town, and set up camp. There was a pile of wooden ammo boxes in the yard, and I used part of them for a bed and part of the lids for shutters on the windows, as there was no glass in them. I've seen more comfortable homes, but I was able to get by. I had a few dollars left, so I got a few groceries at the store. I found the employment office, and checked in every day while I was there.

One day while I was there I heard some little kids playing cowboys and Indians out in the yard. I just happened to have my old 32-40 deer rifle with me, so when I heard them sneaking up to attack the house, I was armed and ready. I think they were a little surprised when they came running in the door and I was standing there with that rifle in my hands. We visited for a while, and I never saw them again. However, the next day their daddy showed up at my door, and gave me a couple dollars to tide me over. I tried not to take it, 'cause I had gotten good news from the employment office that day, and I still had more than a dollar left, but he insisted, so I took it. I never saw him again.

The next day, while I was waiting for the folks that were going to put me to work, I was sitting beside the road on my bedroll with my rifle across my lap, and playing my guitar, when the county sheriff stopped by, and told me the rifle would look better if I stuffed it in the bedroll, so I did what he told me.

A few minutes after he left, I reached down and picked up a piece of paper that was folded up beside me. It turned out to be a dollar bill. I still have that dollar bill, folded just like I found it, almost fifty years ago.

Raymond and Betty Jones showed up not too long after that, and I spent the next three months working for them. They had a little dairy about six miles out of Durango, on what they call the "Florida Mesa". They were hard working people, and I tried to hold up my end.

They didn't leave the farm too often, but they did take a trip to Mesa Verde National Park one time. They took me along, and I sure enjoyed going through the big museum and old Indian ruins.

I stayed on this job til we got the first cutting of hay in the stack, and decided to move on to greener pastures. I was only getting ninety dollars a month, and my brother,

Clifford, had told me that the job he had in Oregon paid two hundred fifty dollars a month.

I jumped in my car and headed North again. I decided to take the scenic route, and headed into Wyoming. My car broke down in Kemmerer, Wyoming, and I never did get it fixed right. Something went wrong in the right-hand front brake cylinder, and I probably couldn't afford the parts, so we just bent the line double and crimped it, and it was like that when I sold it a year or two later.

I went on up into the Yellowstone Park and spent a couple days looking at the sights up there, then headed West. Just inside the west entrance to the park, there were a couple of girls and a boy close to my own age, hitchhiking. I can't remember just what happened, but it turned out that the boy caught a ride with someone else, and the girls got in with me. They were wanting to go to Virginia City, which was a hundred or so miles North of there. It was a few miles out of my way, but I wasn't in any hurry, so I took them on up there. Then I headed West for Summerlake Oregon. It was a fairly uneventful trip, except on one stop I made near Abert Lake. That was the only time in my life I ever stomped a rattlesnake to death with my boot heel. That's the only weapon I had handy. I got to Summerlake and went to work helping Clifford and an older man named Dave put up hay for the rest of the summer. We had a good time working together.

That summer I learned how to sew sacks on an old pull-type combine. I had a kind of stool that I sat on, and when the hundred pound gunny sacks got full, I put them on a chute that held four sacks. When the chute got full, I'd trip a lever and the sacks would slide out on the ground for us to pick up later. Them sacks were sure heavy to throw up on the flat-bed trailer we used to haul them on. That's a lot different from the big combines they use nowadays.

When we finished up the heavy work that fall, and I wasn't needed any more, I took a few days and went over the Cascade Mountains to Sweethome, Oregon. To visit with my old friends, the McDonald family They had moved there a few years before, that, when their Daddy died. We had a nice visit, and talked over old times. Then I went down home for the winter.

I don't think I worked too much that winter, 'cause I can't remember what I did.

I do remember that we did start up our big country band of musicians, called the "Rocking Cowboys". There was a feller down there that kinda influenced this endeavor. He was Audrie Garcia's brother, Arland Penrod. He was a pretty good musician, and had tried to show my sister, Agnes, a few chords on the guitar. I kinda watched from a distance, and I figured out a few chords, too. I think this was a year or two earlier, but I will mention it, anyhow.

Anyway, Buddy and Audrie had moved back from Willcox by the time I got back that fall. He had also learned a few chords on a guitar, so we got the idea that we could combine all this valuable musical talent into a big-time country band. We also enlisted the talents of Tommy Hill, from up in Bisbee, who knew a couple chords, but was a pretty good singer. He did the biggest part of our vocalizing.

We practiced pretty hard for a few months, alternating practice sites from our place to Buddie's, in order to give each family a rest, so they wouldn't climb the walls. We practiced at least twice a week 'til we thought we were ready for our first big gig.

We played for a dance down at the Frontier Clubhouse, and we did pretty good, although we didn't set the world on fire. We weren't quite ready for Nashville, you might say. We went ahead and practiced for a few weeks more, but by then it was time for me to go back to Colorado and Oregon for the spring and summer. I guess I kinda left them high and dry, 'cause I was the only one that could play any lead at all. Anyhow, I had to get back to a paying job,'cause our music wasn't doing it.

I can't remember exactly which rout I tool back to Durango, but I went back up and worked for about three months for the Jones family again.

I met a young feller the year before at a grange dance, that was about the best musician I've ever got acquainted with. His name was Rudy Selph, and he sure could play the guitar. I bumped into him one day, and learned that he was playing music in a bar in downtown Durango. We were both too young at the time to be in a bar without a chaperon, but we were able to use the female vocalist's mother as a chaperon. I would go down and listen to their music twice a week.

One night we were sitting at the table and the band members were having a break.

This well dressed man came over and introduced himself to Rudy as Lefty Frizzel's manager. I sat and listened to the conversation and the questions he asked. He would have hired Rudy on the spot, until he asked if he could read music. When Rudy said no, he explained that there would be times that reading music would be required, so he couldn't give him the job.

Not long after that, something happened with the band or his personal life. I never knew what happened. Anyhow, he came to me one day and asked me to take him to Pagosa Springs. I said sure, and late that evening I took him over there.

He said he was on his way to upper New York State, He must have had a music job there, I guess. He said he would find me a job up there if I wanted to go there. I went along with the idea, and said I would.

It wasn't too long til I got a letter from him saying to come on up, he had me a job on a dairy up there. I had given the Jone's notice and was almost ready to leave, when things went gunnybag. Over the Fourth of July weekend I took Millie Krebbs (the female vocalist in the band) and her girlfriend over the Wolf Creek Pass, East of Pagosa Springs, to Monte Vista. We had a nice trip over there, but on the way home, on top of the pass I tried my brakes, and didn't have any. I might have tried to let myself off the mountain by gearing down, if I'd been alone. But with passengers, I wouldn't chance it. There was a highway maintenance station on top of the pass, so I asked a truck driver to let me off the hill with his truck. I can imagine my little yellow Nash Rambler convertible, towing that big old truck off the mountain, was quite a sight. We made it off safe and sound, anyhow.

We eased our way back to Durango with only one close call. I had to hit the ditch once, trying to miss a cow. The ditch was pretty level, so it didn't do any damage.

I was on my way to the shop to get the brakes fixed a day or two later: came up to an intersection too fast, and couldn't stop without using reverse. This screwed up my transmission, and I was afoot. I was too broke to fix it, and didn't want to hitchhike to New York, so opted to hitchhike to Summerlake, Oregon instead. I don't remember too much about the rides I had the first hundred or hundred and fifty miles. I remember I caught a ride with a trucker about Moab, Utah. He took me into Salt Lake City and let me off downtown. It's a little tough for a country boy to hitchhike in the middle of a big city, but I somehow got the job done. I was there for several hours, and was waiting at a city bus stop, when some young feller about my age took pity on me and offered me a ride. It was about ten o'clock at night by then, and he had just come out of a movie house. I asked him if he could just get me out of the city, and he said he would. I started in telling him about some of my experiences, and he became so fascinated that he took me clear up to the other side of Brigham City, which is forty or fifty miles up the road. I was sure glad to be out of that city. I knew I wouldn't catch a ride that late at night (it was at least mid-night) so I found a grassy area in the bar ditch and slept the rest of the night. It didn't take too long to catch a ride the next morning. I was still six or seven hundred miles from my destination. I had a few more interesting experiences before I got to Summerlake, but not too exciting. It was a trip that I'll never forget, anyhow.

It was a fairly uneventful summer after I got to the ranch that year. My brother and old Alvin Weaver got tanked up one day, and accidentally killed one of the ranch saddle horses. They were testing which of the two horses they were riding could out-pull the other. Alvin's horse fell over dead on him, and I think he broke his arm.

I was the only sober one on the ranch, so it was up to me to explain the situation to the boss (Mickey O'Keefe) when he drove up a few minutes after it happened. After I explained, he had me to pull the saddle off, and drag the dead horse off to the pasture with the tractor, while he went in and got drunk with the rest of the crew. These kind of thing only happened on rainy days, when it was too wet to haul hay.

After the hay was in that year, they sent Fred Kaley (a young feller that was working with us) and me, up to the cattle allotment to build a little stretch of fence. A little later on they sent Clifford up to help us.

We had a little wood burning camp stove in the tent we were staying in. Clifford usually got up to build the fire, and used kerosene to help get the fire started. There was also a can of white gas there beside the kerosene bottle. One morning we heard a pretty good explosion, and saw old Clifford putting out the fire in his hair and eyebrows. He had grabbed the white gas instead of the kerosene, and the white gas is very explosive. Outside of Clifford losing a little hair and eyebrows, no harm was done, but he was a little more careful which jug he picked up after that.

After we got that little piece of fence done up there, I went back home for the winter.

The "Rocking Cowboys" were (or seemed to be) glad to see me. They had recruited a new lead guitar picker, Mark Peek, but they allowed as how they could sure use a fiddle player for their band. I had learned a couple of chords, and could almost play a tune on the fiddle, so I figured I qualified.

We tore into practicing, and were even getting a few tunes worked out after a few weeks. It was getting close to New Years, and old Tom had a job lined up playing for a New Year's Eve dance over at Palominas. At the time my little Rambler was still broke down. Clifford and I had towed that thing more than six hundred miles, from Durango to our home down there. I had no wheels, and no way to communicate.

A few days before New Year's, Charlie Boling came over, and said I could go to work at the Empire Ranch over at Sonoita, which is 80 or 90 miles from our old home place. I couldn't turn down a good paying ranch job, so I rode back with him and went to work. I felt bad that I couldn't be at the dance to play, and had no way to let poor old Tommy know, but I had to make a living. A friend of ours from a neighboring ranch happened to attend that dance, and told us that Tommy was pretty upset with the fiddler, but they had a good time anyhow. I guess Buddy Garcia didn't show up either, so I guess just Tom and Mark Peek played.

I didn't see Tom Hill for a quite a while after that. In 1965, we were living in Union, Oregon. The Union stock show and rodeo was going on. While I was walking down the street that day, I ran into old Tom on the main street of Union. We had a nice visit, and I learned that he was doing good riding bulls, and was still singing as a side-line. The next time I saw him was about eight or ten years ago in Wickenburg, Arizona, where he was owner-operator of the Rancher's Bar. I learned that he had quit bull riding, and worked at the business end of the PRCA for a quite a while before moving to Wickenburg. I never saw or heard anything about Mark Peek again.

I saw Buddy Garcia off and on for several years after that. He was still playing music. He moved to Oklahoma about twenty-five years ago. I learned at Charlie's funeral in February of 2000, that Buddy had died on New Year's Day that same year, from a similar cancer to what killed Charlie.

When I got to work on the Empire ranch, my first assignment was to help redo the telephone line from the ranch headquarters to Sonoita, which is about ten miles. I was the designated pole climber. I had never had a pair of pole climbing spurs on, but I felt like I was up to the job.

The first pole I climbed was about thirty feet tall. I climbed right up that baby big as you please and got the insulators put on. When it was time to come down, I couldn't. I couldn't force myself to pull one of them spurs out of that pole. It took quite a while, but they finally got the stock truck, and a long extension ladder, and I was able to come down the ladder. That was the only time I ever froze up on a pole. I did all the climbing on that ten mile line without further incident. We had to change-out all the old wrap-around splices, and put in crimp style splices.

After we got the telephone line done, we started the spring round-up. I even got a string of horses to ride this time. It was kinda fun. We used a calf table, instead of roping and flanking the calves, but it was still a good round-up. We branded close to two thousand calves that spring.

We also helped set up a big stock tank, and a windmill, from the ground up. Pancho Boice, the owner, did all the welding on the stock tank. He and I worked together as top men when we put up the windmill. He was a good guy to work with, and for. It seems like putting the windmill tower together was pretty easy, but putting the fans up was a little scary. It was pretty windy the day we put the fans up, but we managed to get the job done.

While I was working on the ranch, a feller by the name of Glenn Ellis was working there, too. He and I would go to Tucson Gardens, over in Tucson, to dance, about every Saturday night. We had a lot of fun dancing over there.

One night on our way home, we heard a loud scraping noise, so we pulled over and stopped the car. When we got stopped, we looked behind us and saw his gas tank laying in the road. We dragged it off the road, and struck out cross-country for the ranch headquarters. We got there just about time to go to work, 'cause it was about five miles. It didn't slow us down for long. We got her fixed, and were probably back dancing the next week. We had a lot of fun together.

Along in the spring of the year, I had a little run-in with the chore-man on the ranch. He was yelling and screaming at the boss's kids one day, and I called him on it. He went to the boss and tried to get me fired, but it kinda back-fired on him. He ended up leaving, and I stayed a while longer.

I was getting a little fiddle-footed. Four months was a long time to stay on one job, so I decided to head back North again.

I ran into Mike McDonald over home one day, and he thought his uncle, Bill Johnson, up in Springerville, Arizona, might be needing help on the ranch he was running up there. I pulled the plug over at Sonoita, and he and I headed up the road to Springerville. I had somehow conned my sister, Agnes, out of a little 1941 Studebaker car she had. I think I traded her that old Nash Rambler that had never been too dependable.

When we got to Springerville, we went to work for his Uncle Bill. The ranch was a steer ranch, which shipped yearling cattle up from Mexico, and ran them on the good grass all summer, for the weight they would gain.

Our main job the first few weeks we were there was to unload these Mexican cattle from the trucks, and brand them, and herd them to different pastures on the ranch.

We had a few nice distractions from the harder work that we did in our spare time. We had two or three young horses to try to break to ride. It was quite enjoyable to ride them young horses and try to teach them something.

We also practiced our roping skills any time the boss was gone for the day. We had a lot of fun trying to head and heel them Mexican steers. It wasn't something the boss or the owners would have approved, but it was fun.

One day I had this steer lined out down along a fence and was catching up fast. "Old Sleepy", the horse I was on, was giving it everything he had, and I had my loop built to order. (Note: We tied our rope hard and fast to the saddle horn in them days.) I threw that rope loop on that steer, and thought I had him caught. Too late, I noticed that I also had a big stout fence post in my loop. Before I could pull that old Sleepy horse up, the steer ran on through the loop, but the post didn't. That old nylon rope must have stretched ten feet before it snapped and popped me in the back. As soon as I could get that old horse stopped, I got off and rolled on the ground in pain. My whole right side was black and blue for several days after that, and I never had such a whipping in my life. I was always a little more careful where I roped, after that.

Well, I stayed there on that ranch for another week or two, until we got most of the heavy spring work done, and they didn't need me anymore. I left Mike there and headed back to Durango.

When I got to Durango, I stayed about five days, and had a run-in with the boss, and quit the job cold.

I had never been to Canada, so decided to go up there and see what it looked like. I spent a day or two in the Yellowstone Park again on my way up there, and got to see the first bull moose I ever saw.

I went up into Canada for about fifty miles, at a place not too far west of Glacier National Park. I just spent about a day up thee.

I came back down the road a few miles into Montana, and checked in at several ranches to see if I could find work, without any luck.

On one of those ranches, the owner saw my Arizona license plate and asked what part of Arizona I was from. I told him, and he asked me if I knew a certain horse doctor down there. I said I did, and he told me he had gone to vet school with him. Sure is a small world.

Well, I didn't find any work up there, and was running low on cash, so I decided to go back down to Summer Lake and work with Clifford again. I remember coming through Sand Point, Idaho, and Spokane, Washington, and on down highway #395 to Pendleton, Oregon. My car's transmission had been leaking gear oil all the time, but I had been having it filled every 400 miles on the trip. For some reason, I failed to have it filled in Pendleton, which was a mistake that changed my life forever.

I headed down the road from Pendleton, and sure liked the looks of that country around Ukiah, Oregon. I stopped at a cow camp a mile or two west of Ukiah, to look for work, without success. I did get a free meal, 'cause it was lunch-time.

I headed on down the road, and was doing pretty good 'til I got a few miles east of Mitchell, Oregon. My transmission started making loud noises, and I knew I was in bad trouble. I coasted the last miles into Mitchell, to try to save the transmission. I stopped at the Standard gas station to get transmission oil. This nice feller at the station filled my transmission, and I headed on toward Summer Lake. I got about ten or twelve miles farther down the road, and knew the transmission was too far gone to salvage. I turned around and coasted as far as I could, and limped the old car back into Mitchell, and there I was.

The old feller at the service station let me park my car by the station, and I spent the night there.

The next morning he had me go up into the mountain and get a load of old rotten sawdust, and spread it on the new lawn he had just planted beside the station. This feller was Clarence Jones.

Later that day he introduced me to a feller by the name of Morris De Lisle. He was a hay hauler, and was needing help, so I went to work for him.

Some of the boys that helped us that summer were Jay Cox, Steve Payne, and Jimmy Damron. There were more, but I don't recall their names. We hauled a lot of hay that summer and kinda made a game of it to relieve the misery.

De Lisle made arrangements for some of us to stay at the C-C ranch headquarters with the Bohlke family. He paid Mrs (Hattie) Clarence Bohlke to feed us and we stayed in the bunkhouse at night. Bohlkes were real nice people, and sure treated us good.

I did spend a few weeks batching down at the Burnt Ranch for a while. One day I was down there, and a car drove up and a couple of familiar faces got out and came over where I was at. It was Pat McDonald and his younger brother, Eddie, from over at Sweet Home. They had seen my car sitting at the service station and recognized it. They stayed on and helped us haul hay for a while after that. It was good to see my old friends.

When the haying season was over, I decided to stay on for a while. The sheepherder had come up a few hundred (two hundred) head short on the sheep tally, so I hired on to help Keith Carpenter, one of the cowboys, gather them sheep. It was twenty miles back in the hills to where they thought they had lost them, so we loaded up a pack-horse with some groceries to last a week or so, and our bedrolls, and saddled our horses and headed off to find them sheep. We spent the first night out under the stars, and spent the other three or four nights we were out, in a cow camp house.

We hunted every nook and cranny of that country for four or five days, and only found five head of sheep. It was getting on toward Saturday night, and there was a dance that night, so we broke camp and rode back to headquarters. We learned when we got back that the sheepherder had missed a couple knots on his tally rope, and there weren't any sheep missing at all.

We went to the dance that night, and had a good time, and took a truck back up the next day and got the five sheep we had corralled. That was the only time I ever had any dealings with pack-horses, and I really enjoyed them few days.

Well, the only work the company had for me to do after that trip was herding sheep. One of their herders had quit. I had the idea that I was a cowboy at that time, and not a sheepherder, so I turned it down.

I decided to head South for the winter. It was a little tough to do 'Cause I had developed a one sided attraction for Vernita Bohlke, Clarence's daughter, but I went anyway.

When I got back down home I took a trip over to the Empire Ranch, to try to get back on. Pancho was gone to Denver to a convention for a week, but his wife said I was welcome to stay till he got back, if I wanted to. I didn't happen to have my bedroll with me, so I declined the offer.

I went back to work at the cotton gin for a little while, but wasn't too happy there.

I got to wondering what the country down in Florida looked like, and thought it might be a good place to spend the winter. I jumped in the old 1950 Chevy I had bought from Clarence Jones in Mitchell that summer, and hit the road.

Somewhere North of San Antonio, Texas, I picked up a hitchhiker. He was a soldier on leave from the Army, and hadn't been home for several months. His home was in Corpus Christi, and his wife had a new baby that he had never seen.

I was getting a little tired of driving by then, so I let him do the driving. He sure put that old Chevy through her paces, and we covered that hundred and fifty or so miles in nothing flat.

After I left the soldier-boy off, I drove through some real pretty country, til I got down around Tampa, Florida. I commenced to looking for work, but didn't have any luck. I spent three or four days going to every farm and ranch and horse farm, from Tampa to St. Augustine, and points in between, and couldn't find work.

By this time I was getting a little nervous. I only had less than a hundred dollars with me when I left home, and I had sure used more than half of it. I figured I'd better head for home.

I had always wanted to go to the Grand Ole Opry, and I knew that Nashville was north of Florida somewhere, so I headed north.

I got to the outskirts of Atlanta, Georgia about dark, and rolled out my bedroll for the night. After a good night's sleep, I was laying with my head under the tarp, and heard a car drive up. When I stuck my head out, there was a State Trooper standing over me. I guess someone had called in worried about what I was doing there. I guess most people in that part of the country weren't used to something like that. Anyhow, he didn't bother me, and I went on about my business. I got down the road about five miles (right in downtown Atlanta,) and a motorcycle cop pulled me over. He had noticed my Oregon license plates, and wondered what I was doing so far from home, I guess. He and I visited for a little while, and I was on my way.

I drove on up through the Carolinas, and spent that night just on the edge of the Smokey Mountains National Park in Tennessee.

That night was the first time I remember hearing Hank Snow's song "Miller's Cave". I sure did like that song. Also, that was the night that I heard on the news that Johnny Horton, another one of my favorite singers, had been killed in a car wreck somewhere in Texas.

The next day was a Saturday, and I was sure anxious to get to Nashville. I drove across the Great Smokey Mountains Park, and got into Nashville along about mid-afternoon. Being a country hick, I got a little nervous driving around a big city like Nashville. Finally, I got lost down there somewhere, and all I wanted in Nashville, was out. I ended up somewhere West of town at a complex of buildings where all the people walking around the sidewalks had a vacant look in their eyes. I was afraid if I stopped, they might want me as a resident, so I high-tailed it out of there.

I finally found a main road heading West, and never looked back. I guess I didn't want to see the Grand Ole Opry as bad as I thought.

I drove back across the Mississippi River at Memphis, and spent the night in a cotton field just west of West Memphis, Arkansas. I came on across the southern part of Oklahoma the next day, and spent the next night somewhere between Lubbock, Texas, and Carlsbad, New Mexico.

The next day I spent most of the day touring Carlsbad Caverns. A friend of Clifford's that I had met when they were working together at the "Wonderland of Rocks" in southern Arizona, was the tour guide that day. His name is Dick Stansbury. We had a nice visit, (note, in the late 1980's I worked with a feller that was working with Dick in Mt. McKinley National Park in Alaska, when he retired) Like I said, "It's a small world"

From Carlsbad, I headed home. I made my last gas stop in Deming, New Mexico, and had enough gas to get home on. I had fifty cents in my pocket when I got home, not counting that folded up dollar bill I had found in Durango. I was saving that for real emergencies. It was a good trip.

I didn't stay around home for long. Pat McDonald was down in that country for some reason, and had forty or fifty dollars in his pocket, getting moldy. I still had two dimes to rub together, also. Anyway, Pat had a cousin over in Brawley, California, that worked at one of those big cattle feed-lots over there. Pat thought we might get a job if we went over there. He had the money, and about all I had was time, so we headed that way.

We got over there, and I don't think we even found his cousin, but we checked in at every feed-lot from El Centro to Bakersfield, and a lot of ranches besides, and couldn't find a job. We were in the area three or four days and ate a lot of nineteen cent hamburgers before we gave up.

For some reason I thought we might find some kind of work up at Summer Lake or Mitchell. We stopped at Summer Lake, and Clifford didn't know of any work around, but he did tell us he was going to go down home for Christmas in a week or two. We went on to Mitchell, and sure-enough, Morris DeLisle had about a week's work for both of us, hauling hay from Twinkenham to Mitchell, which is about twenty miles. We got his hay hauled, and he gave us enough money to get back to Summer Lake.

I left my car at Summer Lake and we rode back down home with Clifford. That's where Pat and I parted company, I think Clifford and I went back to Oregon about New Years, or a little after. (I covered a lot of country in the year of 1960)

During the winter of 1960-1961, while I was staying with my folks on Frontier Road, between some of my road trips, a blue pickup drove up in the front yard. A husky old man got out on the driver's side, and Mrs. McCormick, a long time friend of our family, got out on the passenger side. As they approached the house you could see that the old man had one eye missing. My Dad recognized the old feller right off the bat, and introduced him to the rest of the family.

His name was John Power, and he had lost that eye in one of the deadliest shoot-outs in Southeast Arizona history. It was more deadly than the gunfight at the OK corral in Tombstone, but not nearly as publicized.

In 1918, It seems that John, his dad, Tom Power SR, and his brother, Tom, and an old feller by the name of Tom Sisson, were working a mine northwest of Klondyke, Arizona (about fifty or sixty miles northwest of Willcox) in the Galiuro Mountains. About daylight one morning the horses in the corral near the house started acting up. The old man Power, thinking there might be a lion out there, grabbed his rifle and stepped out the door to check. When he got outside, somebody called for him to put up his hands. He leaned his rifle against the door-jam and did as he was told. About that time, they shot him down in cold blood.

When John and young Tom heard the shot, they grabbed their rifles and started shooting back, not even knowing who was out there. When the smoke cleared, three lawmen lay dead out in their yard and their Daddy was dying.

When the boys went out in the yard and saw who they had been shooting at, they knew they were in bad trouble. The High Sheriff and one of his deputies and another feller they didn't know were laying dead in their yard and they knew they would be just as dead if they were apprehended. Nobody would believe it was self-defense. They didn't even know at the time that the posse had just come out to arrest them for draft evasion. They didn't know at the time that one of the lawmen had survived and gone for help, either. They just knew they had to get out of there, and get out fast.

The three of them, John, Tom and Tom Sisson saddled up, and for the next month or so were the subjects of the biggest manhunt in Arizona history. They knew that they would be killed on the spot if they were caught by any Arizona lawmen or posse, so they went down into Mexico. After about a month of running, they gave themselves up to a group of W.S. Calvary men, and survived to stand trial.

They were sentenced to life in prison, and old Tom Sisson, after thirty-five or forty years, died in prison, so he finished his sentence. John and Tom Power had served forty-two years of this term and had been paroled not long before John showed up at our place.

I think that Tom was over in New Mexico working at the time. They were convicted felons and they felt like they were wrongly convicted. As convicted felons, they had no right to petition, so the boys were going around the country asking people to write letters to the Arizona State governor, asking him to pardon them. I wrote several letters the day John was at our house, and different members of our family signed them. It was ten years before they were granted a full pardon, but it happened before they died. About 1970, after reviewing their pardon, John and Tom voted in a general election for the first time in fifty-two years. Tom died less than a week later, but John lived on for a few years. Justice sometimes takes a lot of time.

Daddy knew these boys before they went to prison, and even visited them in prison when he lived up in the Phoenix area. John Power lived with my folks for close to a year after he got out of prison. Tom showed up once in a while, but I was living in Oregon at the time and I never did meet him. They were both interesting characters, I guess. To learn more about these fellers, you can read "Shoot-out At Dawn" written by Tom Power and some other feller.

When I got back to Oregon, I stayed around Clifford's for a day or two, and headed back up to Mitchell. When I got there, I got a job feeding cattle up on Shoo-fly Creek, which is about fifteen miles north of Mitchell. There were three hundred head of cows split into two herds on separate feed-lots a couple miles apart. I fed with a team of horses and would lead the team from herd to herd on a saddle horse. We had a hay wagon at each place. That was the first time I ever worked a team of horses. I also had a couple of half-broke young horses I was working with some. I was doing work that I enjoyed.

Over the hill about five of six miles was the Shawn Ranch, where my straw-boss and working partner lived. He was Al Lowry. We buckaroo'd together that spring.

I had seen a little red-headed girl, that I thought might have been twelve or thirteen years old, over there, and asked Al about her. When he told me she was seventeen, I got a little more interested.

When the cows stopped coming to the feed grounds in the spring, I had to move over to the Shawn Ranch and start helping Al work cattle. I rode one gentle saddle-horse, and led the other three cross-country five or six miles to the Shawn Ranch. We turned the team of work horses out to pasture.

I moved into the basement of the house that Al and Kathy Lowry and their three kids lived in. It was here that I got to meet the little red-headed girl. A day or two after I got there, she came over one evening, and they introduced her as Cam Scott. One of the first things I said to her was that I had ridden horse-back for forty miles to see her a day or two before that, but she wasn't home. Another thing I said in the course of the evening was that I would take her to Hawaii some day. The first statement was a little exaggerated, but the second statement came true about fourteen and a half years later, not long after our fourteenth wedding anniversary.

I started to work with Al Lowry and Ray Critchelo, the ranch manager, taking care of the cow work on the ranch. We branded close to two thousand calves that spring, and I got to do a lot of the roping. I also had three young horses I was working with, and I really enjoyed that. One of the horses bucked me off several times, but I had him going pretty good by the end of spring roundup. The other two horses never gave me too much trouble at all. All and all, it was a fun three or four months.

To add to the fun, I happened to be courting that little red head, who's hair was slowly turning back to brown, which I liked a lot better. We had a lot of fun times, too. She had moved to Dayville that spring, which was about forty-five miles from where I was working. Finally, along about the middle of July, we got hitched, to save wear and tear on my poor old Chevy car.

I was back working with Morris DeLisle by then and we sure hauled a lot of hay that summer. I think it was something like a hundred and thirty five thousand bales. I loaded almost every one of them. We went through a lot of men that summer, but I stayed to the end of the season.

After haying season, I went back to work for Hudspeth Ranches up at Antone. Bob Peterson was the head-man up there. I worked through the fall of the year, and thought I was set for life, but things don't always work out that easy.

We had gone to town and spent a good bit of money on Christmas things about a week before Christmas. The next day Bob came by the house and told me I was laid off for the winter. He said he would like to hire me back in the spring when work picked up. They let us stay in the house for the winter.

We coasted along through the cold winter months, and got by. It was a cold winter. Along in February after some of the snow had gone off, I got me a gold pan and spent a lot of time up in

Spanish Gulch. The old timers had taken a lot of gold out of that canyon. I messed around up there for several days, and one day came up with two or three small flakes of gold in my pan. I rushed home and told the little Missus that I thought we were probably set for life, 'cause I knew there was a lot more where that came from. I panned there a quite a bit more, but didn't find more than a few flakes.

By this time I'm sure the little lady was having second thoughts about her choice of a mate. So I decided to look for something a little more lucrative. I knew my brother, Charlie, was working in the underground mines in Bisbee, Arizona, and thought he might help me get a job there. We gathered up our few belongings and hit the trail for Southeastern Arizona.

When we got there we stayed with my folks until we could get on our feet. They always took care of us kids.

I did a little part-time work while I waited to go to work in the mines, but not too much. Finally, I got a job working over at the Cole shaft in Bisbee, on the eleven and twelve hundred foot levels. The first trip down that shaft was a quite a thrill. That cage goes down almost like a free-fall, but you get used to it.

After I worked there for about three months, our oldest son, Jimmy, was born on the fourteenth of June. By then, my folks were building us a new house, and had just put the roof on it. On the day he was born, the new roof blew off the house while my folks were working on it. Momma got a bruise on her leg, but it could have been worse.

Cam had to stay in the hospital for several days because the baby was born by c-section. I had to be a little evasive when she would ask how the house was coming along, so she didn't find out til she got home from the hospital. They got it fixed back up and we were living in the house before too long.

I had a few close calls in the year I worked in the mine that influenced my decision to not make a career of underground mining. There's a lot of dangers down there. The miners always work in pairs in the mine, for safety reasons. The new workers, known as muckers, fill in when a miner's partner is gone for a shift. One night I was working in a stope with a Mexican named Joe Valenzuela, nicknamed "Roley Poley". (Lots of miners had nicknames.) He and his partner had moved from another stope not too long before this.

We were running short on vent-tubing. (a flexible rubberized nylon pipe that they use to blow air into the working areas.) He asked me if I would go back to the old worked-out stope and bring back some of the pipe they had left there. I got up and was almost out of the stope when he called me back. He said he would get it tomorrow when his partner got back.

The next night about the middle of the shift, I was working in the drift with another feller, and someone came by and said that "Roley Poley" was dead. He had gone back in that old worked-out stope to get that vent pipe, and died in a pocket of dead air (air completely devoid of oxygen.) I guess you can say he crossed the great divide in my place. It just wasn't my time yet. I had too many rivers to cross.

I stayed working in the mines til my first year was up, and decided to go back to Mitchell. We had our little house paid for by then, and money in the bank.

I have to add here, that without the best two parents in the world, this story would have never been written. My folks helped us every way they could.

We went on back to Mitchell, and I went back to work for Morris DeLisle. We built a little fence while we waited for the hay to get ready. Then we hauled hay for the rest of the summer. After the haying season was over. I spent most of the winter working for Hudspeth Ranch, down at the C-C. I helped feed cattle and helped build quite a bit of fence that winter. This experience would prove valuable down the road a piece.

We had an experience that year that did cause us some concern. There were a couple of house cats that DeLisle had left at the house we bought from him when we got back from Arizona. (Which we paid cash for, by the way) with earnings from my year in the mines. Not too many people are able to buy and pay for two homes in one year. (the mines were good to us.)

Our little boy, Jim, liked to chase them cats. He was learning to walk good at this time. We usually watched him pretty close. This day I was working in my garden. I guess I forgot he was out there, or he came out without me knowing. I guess Cam thought he was with me.

I went in the house for a drink or something, and there was no Jim. We got real worried, and went all around the neighborhood looking for him, and recruited all the neighbors to help us find him. One of our neighbors found him sitting on a hundred foot high cliff about a hundred yards from our house. I guess he had fallen about three feet and had hung up on a bush, or would have ended up at the bottom of that cliff.

We knew he had chased one of those cats down there, so I eliminated the first cat I saw. I had cooled down enough when the other cat showed up, that I let him live, but we sure kept a close eye on our little boy after that.

The next year, 1964, I decided to branch out on my own. When haying season started, I took a contract to haul hay for the Collin's boys Phopiana Ranch, and for Fran Cherry's Ranch. I used their equipment, and got a nickel a bale to haul it. I hired the two Huddlesten boys, Tommy 16, and Eddie, 14, to help me. Eddie drove the tractor and helped us unload hay, and Tommy and I loaded it. We hauled quite a bit of hay that year, and I made better money than I could make working for wages. Toward the end of the haying season, I saw an ad in my Farm Bureau insurance booklet, for a ten acre apple orchard for sale. I thought that being an orchardist might be more fun than hauling hay so I went over and had a look.

It wasn't too long before we were living in Union, Oregon on that ten acre apple orchard, plus three acres of grass. It was a real nice place. I had to sell both our homes to get the down payment, but I figured it was worth it. I sold our home in Arizona to my brother, Charlie, and the one in Mitchell to Clarence Bohlke. I needed a job to make the payments, so I got a job hauling hay and other odds and ends a mile or two out of Union. I also worked one day a week at the LaGrande Livestock Auction sale yard on sale days. Along late in the fall my ranch job ran out, so I was down to one day a week at the sale yard. It didn't cover our bills too good.

About that time I was helping doctor a calf, or yearling, actually, when the calf flung his head and smashed one of my fingernails off between his horn and the chute. The owner, Bob Greene, took me to the emergency room and had it doctored for me. On the way to the hospital I explained my situation, and he put me on working steady. I helped haul hay and helped feed the cattle in the sale yard pens. That kept us going for the winter.

Little Jim also had a pleasant surprise that year at Christmas time. We came home from somewhere on Christmas Eve, and there was a nice big ham laying there in the house. The feller I had worked for earlier that fall had left it for us. A little later in the evening we heard a knock on the door. When we opened the door, there stood Old St. Nick with a bag of toys and a big turkey. He gave Jim some nice presents, and visited for a while, and was on his way. Our good neighbors across the street had told him about us, I guess. He was taking toys around the town to needy people, and I'm sure we qualified.

Another thing I did that winter was to sing on the radio for about three months or more. The radio station was having a charity (24 hour show) marathon and needed local talent to do the singing and what-not. I did a little singing at that time, so I went down with my guitar and taped a few songs, thinking it might attract some musical group that could use some help. Sure-enough, a feller by the name of "Shorty, the Drifting Cowboy", who had a half-hour show three times a week on that radio station (KLRM in LaGrande) asked me to be a guest star on his radio show. I played and sang on that show every session for more than three months. I was working in LaGrande anyhow at the sale yard, so it wasn't far out of my way. I never received any monetary compensation for my talent, but did have an enjoyable experience.

That was the year of the 1964 Christmas flood, and it flooded again in January 1965. They said it was the worst flood that the Northwest had seen in a hundred years.

I finally got a job at the sawmill in Union, and that ended my big-time singing career. My sawmill job paid a lot better anyhow.

A few days before our fourth wedding anniversary our daughter, Glenda, was born. She was a real prize, and still is today.

I stayed with the sawmill job a little more than a year and decided to move on. I had leased the apple orchard out on a percentage of the crop, and it paid it's own way in 1965. but the frost killed the fruit buds in 1966, and I couldn't lease the orchard out. We sold the orchard to the owner of the lumber company I worked for, and hit the trail to Alaska. I had some kinfolks and friends working up there and thought I could get work up there.

We loaded up what we didn't sell of our belongings into our pickup truck, and headed up the Alaska Highway. It took us about a week to get to Anchorage without any serious problems.

We stayed with my sister, Peggy for a few days and then rented a little place for a month.

I had been kinda promised a job by my brother-in-law's brother, so I didn't look for work too hard. His job did not materialize by the end of the month, so we got nervous and loaded up and came back to Oregon.

We had a little car trouble coming down the Alaska Highway. A tie-rod end came off and almost put us in the ditch. I found a piece of wire and wired it back on. We creeped on into White-Horse, Yukon Territory, and got it fixed. We had another problem a few hundred miles down the road, but I don't remember what it was.

Glenda, our baby, was sick, and we couldn't find a place to stay for a couple days (all the motels were filled up because of a Canadian holiday week-end.)

When we got back to Oregon, I left the Missus and the little ones over at her mother's place near Pendleton and found a new home for us to buy back in Mitchell, Oregon. (New to us, anyhow.)

The next three years were some of our best; fishing in the spring and summer (Jim always seemed to catch the biggest fish,) hunting in the fall, and playing in the snow in the winter. There was also music to play.

When we got settled in our new home I got a job with Tom Silvey, a gypo logger in the area. I bumped knots on the landing for three or four months, till it got too muddy to log.

During this period of time, we almost lost our little Jim twice. One day he disappeared for a quite a while and we couldn't find him. We looked everywhere and were getting panicky. Finally one of us thought to look in an old wooden trunk upstairs in the house, and he was in there taking a nap (the lid was closed.)I don't know how long he had been in there, but I'm sure he didn't have much air left.

Not long after that he got scarlet fever and we had to rush him to the hospital in Prineville. It sure tore us up to leave the little feller screaming in the hospital that night, but I had to work the next day. He sure was glad to see us a couple days later when we went to pick him up.

After Tom laid me off I went to work for Hudspeth Sawmill Company, piling brush ahead of their road crew. This job lasted til the snow got too deep, and I picked it up in the spring after the snow went off.

1967. I worked there a month or two longer and had a chance to go to work for the State Highway Department, and took it. I worked there for almost three years before I got my next wild hair.

In this time period we had some good experience and bad.

Fred Fitzgerald was a pretty good guitar picker, and got the idea that he and I should start up a country band. He had a young friend in Prineville, a girl named Marci Copeland. We could use her as our main vocalist, 'cause she was wanting to be a musician, too.

We practiced a lot and got to where we were able to play for a few dances. We named our band "Marci and Outlaws". We had a lot of fun for a couple of years.

Things started going sour, so I encouraged Marci to find another group to sing with. She joined a group of professional musicians, and toured all over the country for several years. She married one of the musicians. The last time I saw Marci was when I was running my restaurant two or three years later. She and her folks stopped by and we had a nice visit. I haven't seen or heard from any of them since.

The "Outlaws" went on without her and replaced her with Joe Fitzgerald's wife, Evelyn. Joe started playing bass, and they played for many years around the area. I stayed a short time after Marci left, and bailed out gracefully.

Things went along pretty good for a couple years after we came back from Alaska. Sometime during this time period, I bought an old building in town that would later become our restaurant. It was a real mess when we bought it, but we got it cleaned up and usable before long.

The young people in Mitchell didn't have any place where they could hang out and visit, so I decided that old building would make a nice recreation hall. The feller that ran the local bar had connections with people that had pool tables and stuff, and would set them up on a percentage of the receipts. I threw in with him and we got two pool tables, a shuffle-board, and a jukebox set up. The kids had a place to recreate. I think they really enjoyed it.

Things went along pretty smooth until the fall of 1969. when things happened that shouldn't have happened, and things were a little shakey for a while. We worked things out, and by the time spring rolled around, I was ready for a new adventure. Highway work was a little boring.

Dick and Agnes, my sister and brother-in-law, were planning to go back to Alaska from Arizona that spring, and said I could get a job with the fence company that Dick worked for up there in the summertime. I knew that they payed high wages up there, so decided to go.

I don't know why, but we sold our house before we went back up there.

I gave notice at the job, and when Dick and Agnes came through on their way up there, I traveled with them in my little blue V.W. Bug we had at the time. I left the wife and kids there in Mitchell to come up after school was out. Our oldest boy, Jim, was in school by then.

I kinda left Dick and Agnes in my dust on the way up the Al-Can Highway 'cause I was traveling light, and they had their little baby, Paula, with them and had to stop more often.

We got to Anchorage and my first assignment when I went to work was a guardrail job over on the Canadian border. I worked with a six-man crew, including one of the owners of the company, Jack McDonald, who was my sister Peggy's brother-in-law.

We used the first fifth-wheel trailer in Anchorage, Alaska for our living quarters. After a few days, I was designated cook, 'cause I was the only one in camp that could boil water without scorching it. I even got off from work a half hour or so early to tend to the cooking. The meals were not always gourmet, but we survived for a couple months on them.

We up-graded the old guardrail (changed out the old rail and put in new,) from the Canadian border to Delta Junction. Another crew worked from Delta Junction on into Fairbanks. It was a good duty. After about six weeks, the wife and kids flew up.

Over time, after the wife and kids had gotten to Anchorage, I had a close call with a moose. I was driving back and forth to Anchorage on weekends by then, although we only had one day off. I would get home about midnight Saturday night, and leave about midnight on Sunday night. It was about three hundred miles to the job.

This trip I had the boss's boy with me and was really hitting the high spots on our way back to the job. I saw what I thought was a hitchhiker, standing on the side of the road, about a quarter mile away. (I was a little sleepy and not seeing too good.) I got less than a hundred yards from him and he turned into a big old moose headed across the road in front of me. If I would have hit the brake instead of the gas peddle, we would have both been killed. That old moose slobbered on my car and fell down in the road as we went by. Sure was a close call, but we made it.

After we finished the border job, we spent a few days up around Willow, not too far north of Anchorage, and then flew into Nome for our next big job. We had a lot of fun in Nome.

The first week we were there, we couldn't work, 'cause we didn't have a post-hole digging machine that would work. We had to have one flown in from Anchorage. We spent some time driving around the area (there was not more than fifty or sixty miles of roads in the whole area.) We took an unguided tour through one of the biggest bucket-line gold dredges in the world at the time. It had shut down about eight years earlier, and was sitting there vacant. It sure was interesting. I even bought a gold pan and panned a little dirt on the beaches of Nome, but didn't get any gold.

We also spent our evenings that week in the Board of Trade Bar, a few blocks from where we were staying, to listen to the good country band that was playing there. They were the Carroway Brothers, straight out of Nashville, Tennessee. They played there six nights a week. One night one of the boys broke a guitar string on his guitar and didn't have a spare. I ran over to the hotel where we were staying and got him a string out of my guitar case. After that, every time I went in there, they would have me up on stage singing a few tunes. They even gave me one of their records, which I still have. It was a real fun month or so.

When we finished the job in Nome and got back to Anchorage, it was about time for school to start. I had given up on any thoughts of permanent residence in Alaska, so I made a phone call to "Doc" Marsh in Mitchell, Oregon and bought us a house to move back to. I put the wife and kids on the plane, and they were there in time for Jim to go back to school that fall.

I stayed on for several more weeks and got home about the middle of October. I flew down and shipped my car back on the ferry. Dick and Agnes and I had shipped our cars on the same day, but somehow my car had gotten on an earlier barge. We flew down together, and my little V.W. Bug was waiting for me. Dick and Agnes were a little upset when they learned that their car wouldn't be there for a few days.

I took them to a motel and helped them get settled in, waved good-bye, and came on back to Mitchell.

A few days later, when they stopped by on their way back to Arizona, they were still on speaking terms. (Really, we all had a good laugh and they went on about their business. None of my family has ever taken life too serious.)

When I got back to Mitchell, Mel Beachy, the foreman, reinstated me on my old highway job. We were set for the duration, or thought so anyhow.

About tis time, I was a little disillusioned with our recreation hall, and decided to sell the building to someone that could make a better use of it. A feller by the name of Roy Fuller, from over around Portland, made a down-payment on it and put in a restaurant. He ran the restaurant for a few months, and decided he wasn't quite up to the task, so decided to sell it, giving me first choice at it. I bought it back, paying him for his equipment, and canceling the mortgage. I was in the restaurant business.

My total experience in cooking was the couple months I batched in Shoo-Fly Canyon where I fed cattle, and the few weeks of cooking for the guardrail crew in Alaska, so I needed a few instructions. He took a couple hours to show me how to make gravy and a few other basics, and I was on my way.

I was working steady for the highway department, so I needed a manager. I hired Ruth Fitzgerald, (Fred's wife) and we made that place pay from the day we moved in. She was a real lifesaver. I knew that we had to make every move count in a new business, so I put on an apron and helped every evening, and carried the whole weekend alone. We worked alone because there wasn't enough business to afford a second person. Customers were usually very patient.

My wife was pregnant with our youngest son, David, until September 8th that year, and then she had a full time job changing diapers and other baby things, so wasn't able to help much.

We kept the place open til about Thanksgiving that year and closed down for the winter. I was afraid it wouldn't pay it's way.

The next year in April we opened back up, and did a good business all summer. I was getting a little weary by then, so I leased the place out to a feller I was working with, and his wife. There was living quarters upstairs over the restaurant.

I have to back up a little bit, but I need to say that we had a nice trip to Disneyland that spring before we opened the restaurant back up. The two older kids enjoyed it almost as much as we did, but David was still a little too young to care. We went back several times after that, so he got his chance too. Disneyland is not too far out of the way on our way down to Arizona where I was raised. I still try to get down there as often as I can (not to Disneyland, but down home.)

1970-1973 Along sometime in this time frame, I decided that I wanted to move out of town. We had purchased a five acre lot about five miles out of town. It had an old house on it that everybody thought I should burn down. I got to looking at it and decided I should remodel it instead.

I grabbed my old chain saw and a claw hammer (the only tools I owned) and started remodeling. I took all the vacation time I had coming, and some I didn't, and remodeled that old house. I wasn't the prettiest job of remodeling you ever saw, but when I got through with the job, we had a livable home. We lived there for three or four years, and sold out. As near as I know, somebody is still living in that old house, more than thirty years later. Beat heck out of burning it down. I don't always listen to well-meaning advice, you might say.

Things went along pretty smooth for a few years after we leased the restaurant out. I stayed with the highway department for quite a while. My good friend, Mel Beachy, had moved on and some of the new personnel I was working with were not people that I wanted to work with forever, so I started looking for something different.

In this time period, Jim started going deer hunting with me. He would grab his trusty old b-b gun, and we would head for the hills. I let him shoot his b-b gun at an old doe once in a while. One trip I remember well, he saw a nice buck before I did, and said "There's one, Daddy". We had heart and liver for supper that night. We had some good times together.

About this time I started going over to Heppner Mountain hunting elk with Fred and Joe Fitzgerald. I could almost write a book about the fun times we had in elk camp. One of the last things Fred and I talked about when we went to see him on his dying bed, was those elk hunting trips. He died in 1977, We got a Christmas card from Joe and Evelyn the day I am writing this. 12-14-05. They are very good friends.

Along in the spring or summer of 1974 I went to work for Bob Powell, cutting logs. I thought that would be a way to make some big money. Most of the jobs we had were along way from home, and we had to camp all week on his camp trailer. I was designated chef again. I worked for Bob for a few months and only had one serious accident.

Bob was falling the trees and I was bucking them behind him. He felled a bee tree and when I got on it to buck it, I got about fifty bee stings. I had a bad reaction, and he rushed me to the hospital where they gave me a shot of adrenalin and fixed me right up. It sure was a relief.

I had a little falling-out with Bob not too long after that, and pulled the plug.

I gathered up the little family and went down home to Southern Arizona, and spent the winter. I kinda wanted my kids to get acquainted with their grandparents, anyhow. We put the older two kids in school and spent four or five months down there. I helped my sister, Marjie's husband drill water wells that winter. I mostly perforated casing (cut slots in it with a cutting torch) and welding it together when we put it down the well.

Dick Swisher, Agnes's husband, was a superintendent for the Mt. McKinley Fence Company in Alaska, where I had worked before, and said he would get me a job up there the next summer, so I had a job to go to when spring broke.

That winter we had several nice trips around the area down there. We went to Tombstone and spent the day once, and I know we all took a trip the mountains to look for "Curly Bill's" treasure at least once. (We have looked for that treasure off and on for close to fifty years.) We took a nice fishing trip down to Kino Bay, a short distance southwest of Hermosillo, Mexico the last weekend we were there and had a lot of fun. We caught a lot of funny-looking fish, and someone even caught a small octopus.

On our way back to Oregon that spring, we made another trip back to Disneyland, and even David was old enough to enjoy the rides this time. It was a real joy to watch them little fellers and Glenda on some of those rides.

After we left Disneyland we got into a bad snowstorm at Dunsmuir, California. It took us four hours to travel the next twelve miles to Weed, California, where we managed to get the last available room in town, about noon that day. We spent the rest of that day and that night in the honeymoon suite of that motel, to let the storm blow over, but were not able to take advantage of the situation, 'cause the kids were there. The rest of the trip home was mostly uneventful.

My trip to Alaska that year was solo. I flew up to Anchorage, and left the wife and kids to look after our little farm. We almost always had a garden.

When I got to Anchorage, I worked on residential fence in anchorage for a few weeks before going out on the big job. I had the little missus fly up for a few days visit before we went on to Valdez on the big job. We had a nice visit.

Before we (Dick and I) went on down to Valdez, we experienced a fairly strong earthquake in Anchorage. It shook the little camp trailer we were staying in pretty good. I just thought it was Dick getting out of bed, but he knew what it was right away. He had been through some quakes before, but I think he missed the big one in 1964. My sister, Peggy, went through that one, and I guess it was pretty scary. I had been through one on my previous trip.

That summer we had some interesting experiences down in Valdez. We built about fourteen thousand feet of nine foot tall chain link fence, on ground that was almost too steep to stand up on in some places. Most of the crew, like myself, had not had much experience with building chain link fence, but we got the job done.

We had a lot of black bears for company on the fence line, and we sure had to keep a close eye on our lunches. I sat down one day to eat lunch, and the other boys on the crew didn't watch their lunches close enough. A little black bear (about two hundred pounds) came over and ate all their lunches. He ate lunch with me instead. When he came over and started sniffing up my leg after dessert, I backed off a step or two, and he went on his way. There were bears in camp, too, and would even go in the barracks where we stayed sometimes.

It would take a lot of paper to describe all the fun and interesting things that happened up there that summer. It was a real enjoyable experience, and I made the best money I ever made in my life.

I decided along towards the end of the job that it would be a good idea to fulfill the statement I made on the day that I met my wife. So I went to a travel agent and made arrangements for she and I to meet on the island of, Oahu, Hawaii.

When the day came, I flew out of Anchorage, and she flew out of Portland, Oregon and met me in Honolulu. She had left our kids with some of our good friends in Mitchell for the week. That was one of the best weeks of our lives.

We had a package deal which included a rental car, and drove all over the island as we pleased. We toured three islands in all, Oahu, Maui, and the big island of Hawaii. There was a lot of pretty and contrasting scenery over there. There are places over there where you can go from rain forest to desert landscape in less then five miles. It would be nice to go back sometime, but our resources are too limited.

At least we had a nice honeymoon that we had missed out on fourteen years earlier. (I had to work the day of our wedding.)

When we got home after our vacation, I think I started doing contract pre-commercial tree thinning for the Forest Service. I know I did that for a year or two after my Alaska trip. I also worked some for Bob Helms, and Jim Phegly, over close to Richmond, on a logging job.

About this time was when we heard some nice sounds coming out of Jim's bedroom. He was teaching himself to play the mandolin. I showed him a couple chords, and he took on his own from there. He still plays a good job of it thirty years later. He also does a good job on the guitar.

Some of our most memorable times were watching the kids play sports. They were all three able to participate, and we enjoyed watching them for many years. That was our main entertainment in them days. We also went to quite a few dances in them days, and danced our legs off. Then there was the hunting and fishing. Jim got his first buck deer during this time. I still spent time over on Heppner Mountain, hunting elk with the Fitzgerald boys, which was always fun.

Things went along pretty smooth for a year or two, and we could almost see the end of the rainbow, when we experienced another set-back. After I made some bad decisions, the worst of which was going in the logging business with Bob Helms. He had some logging equipment, and needed someone with a truck and loader to haul the logs. I was elected.

I made a down payment on a truck and loader and was in the hauling business. It didn't matter that I'd never even been inside a truck or loader in my life. I could learn. You better believe I learned. Due to my total inexperience and other circumstances beyond my control, in less than six months I ended up letting the truck and loader go back, at a financial loss that has never been overcome. I wasn't quite as lucky as I was in the restaurant business, but we moved on.

After that fiasco, I went back to pre-commercial tree thinning for a while. We were doing a pretty good job of catch-up when Lloy Munjar came by and asked me to go to work over at Spray Highway Dept. I had worked for Lloy for several years at Mitchell before he got the foreman job it Spray.

I was a little tired of the snow running down the collar of my coat, off them trees I was cutting, so, (against my better judgment,) I accepted the job.

When I finished the contract I was working on, I started commuting to Spray to work, 'til we could find a place to stay. We even rented a house for a month or two, but didn't stay in it.

We found a nine acre lot for sale, and I think I borrowed on a real-estate contract to buy it. (We had sold one of our houses in Mitchell.)I found a young couple named Dan and Mary Howe, that were looking for their first building contract, to build us a house on this lot. I had a well drilled, and when I was sure I had water, we started our new house. I helped with the building as much as I could in my spare time, and in about four months we moved into our new home. We were set for life.

We settled in for a couple years, and outside of a little run-in with the city fathers, things were going pretty smooth.

We got to meet new friends. We started a new music group "The Bunchgrass Boys and Mary Anne", who's members included Mike Medloc, Ed Kendal, Rick and Mary Anne Seagal, Jim and me. We played for community functions for several years, including election rallies for Vic Atika and Al Ulman. We still enjoy watching our kids play sports.

I was working with a a good crew, and might have stayed with the job for the duration, if gold prices hadn't gone to eight hundred dollars an ounce.

At that time I was involved with my folks and a couple of my siblings in some mining claims in Southern Arizona. I thought I could go down there and get rich mining gold. I quit my state job and went down there and rented a backhoe for a couple months and tried to get a project started. To make a long story short, we did get a company to lease the property for two or three years, but I didn't get rich. We received some advance royalties, but never got into production.

Jim had left Spray and gone back to Mitchell to finish his senior year of school.

He graduated valedictorian of his class, and you can bet that we were proud parents.

After Jim's graduation I decided to take my family back to Colorado and meet some of my old acquaintances, and then go down home for a while. We went to Durango, where I pointed out the place where I had spent the week in that old deserted cabin. There was a nice house in it's place. Then we located Raymond and Betty Janes, who had sold their farm and moved. We had a nice visit and they told me that my old musician friend, Rudy Selph, was back in the area, running a propane gas business. We looked him up, and he and Jim and I had a nice jam session that we recorded on tape. We still have that tape.

From there we went to Pima, Arizona, to visit my brother, Charlie.

We had learned from Rudy that his parents had moved from Durango to Pima not too long prior to this, and we should look them up. We did look them up, and in the course of our conversation that evening, we learned that Rudy had been playing lead guitar for Johnny Horton when Johnny Horton got killed. Rudy was one of the best musicians I ever met, and I've met a lot of musicians.

From Charlie's, we went on down the the folk's place, and spent some time visiting. On our way back to Oregon we went by Disneyland again. David was old enough to really enjoy it this time, and we all had a really good time.

Along in the spring of the next year (1981) Jim started his twenty year career in the Air Force. Glenda got married that spring, also. We moved on.

That summer I got a log-truck driving job over in Heppner. Things went along pretty good for a few months, til I tried to negotiate a curve in the road at too high rate of speed, and wrecked the truck. When the dust cleared, I think I crawled out the broken windshield and hitched a ride back to town. When I explained the situation to the boss, I was once more amongst the unemployed.

To solve my employment problem, I hired on with "Pat" Patterson, a gypo logger from Heppner. Things went along pretty good for a few months, til I locked horns with the jammer (log-loading machine) grapples, and came out second best. I guess it threw me about twenty feet through the air. Everyone that saw it happen thought I was dead, but I fooled them. I don't know how long I was out cold, but when I came out of it, things were pretty quiet around there. I tried to get up, but they insisted they had to carry me to the boss's pickup. They loaded me in, and he took me to a clinic in Heppner, where I got an x-ray. There didn't seem to be any broken bones, but I sure was sore for a couple months.

That happened on Friday, and I went back to work the next Monday, but only worked a few more days before I had a run-in with the boss and went on to greener pastures.

I had been gone from home (Arizona) for close to twenty-five years, and thought it might be nice to go down there and spend some time a little closer to my aging parents. I went down to see if I could find a job to go down there. I did actually work for a couple days on a construction job, til the roller I was running, broke down.

I went over to Rodeo New Mexico, to see Lloyd Mauzy, my old friend from high-school. He had a nice apple orchard, up in the foothills of the Chiricahua Mountains, that needed a caretaker, and his father-in-law, who was a Cochise County Commissioner would have given me a job running road grader in that area. I sure was tempted, but I knew my wife couldn't tolerate the isolation, so I passed on this proposal.

I had another good friend over in Sonoita, from my Empire Ranch days, that I hadn't seen in quite a while, so I went over for a visit. This was Baily Foster. In the course of our conversation, I learned that he was thinking about starting up a pump business. He had some antiquated equipment, and wanted to up-grade, and said he wouldn't mind having a partner. I knew the pump business was a very lucrative business (there's thousands of wells in that area) so I was going to throw in with him. We even checked out prices on pump rigs together. We were almost ready to go to work together, when the subject of school came up. He informed me that the Patagonia School, where David would go to school, was a real rough school. Not wanting to put David in a bad environment, I decided to bunch the project and headed back to Oregon. (Note: Baily Foster started his pump business, and was very successful. I could have been a full partner, but family came first, and still does.)

This is when I started my illustrious career as a barbwire fence builder. This would sustain us for the next twenty odd years.

Rockey Goodell had mentioned before I went South, that he and his neighbor, Dr Tony Sykes, had a boundary fence they wanted to change, so that was my first fence job. I finished that small job and spent the rest of the summer up on Waterman Flat rebuilding many miles of fence for Ben Westlund, who had a ranch up there at that time. He is now a prominent politician in the central Oregon area.

That fall I got my first real good contract. Gary Griffith, a cousin to Don Griffith, a friend of ours in Spray, had taken on this contract and got too busy doing other things to do it, so he asked if I would do it for him. He even let me use his camp trailer to stay in. The job was up at Starkey, more than a hundred miles from home. There was several miles of new fence to build and also several miles to take out and roll up.

Along towards the end of the project, the round-up crew showed up to gather cattle and take them home for the winter. There was eight men in the crew, (nine counting myself). This was another time I had occasion to demonstrate my culinary skills. I was designated chef for the crew. Somehow they all survived.

They were there for about ten days, and I helped them work cows when they needed help. We had a good time and I'm still on a friendly basis with the ones that are still alive.

One day towards the end of the project, I took the day off and went hunting with the owner's kid and some of his friends. This one young feller was kinda laughing 'cause he made a circle onto the neighbor's land that was posted. He thought he was in pretty good shape and it wasn't likely anybody could catch him if they tried.

Somebody in the crew killed a nice spike elk down in the bottom of a real steep canyon. It was more than a quarter mile from the elk to the top of the rim, where we could get the pickup. We got the elk gutted and cut the head off. I grabbed the elk head and my rifle and this young feller got his rifle and we headed up the hill to get the pack-boards. I took the elk head up to the rig and got a pack-board and met him about two thirds of the way up the hill, stopped for a breather. I went down and loaded up the hind-quarters and carried them up to the rig. And went back down about half way and relieved the kid that was packing the rib cage while the other two boys carried the two front legs on up the hill. The young braggart had second thoughts about then. I was more than fifteen years older than any of those boys, but was in pretty good shape at the time.

I think I ended up helping one of them ranchers that were in camp that fall, feed cattle all winter. Larry Wade and his son, Rob, had, and still have, a nice ranch over by Fossil, Oregon, and I helped them.

Things went along pretty good after that first year. I kept enough work ahead to keep the wolf away from the door. Nothing too exciting happened until our son, Jim, announced his wedding plans. To complicate things a little, he planned to get married in England. We wanted to be at the wedding, but were a little strapped for cash, so I cashed out the residual balance on the real-estate contract we had borrowed on to buy our property in Spray, and we were on our way to Great Britain.

We got our passports in Bend, Oregon, and caught a plane out of Vancouver, British Columbia. It was about a nine hour flight from there to Manchester, England, where Jim met us at the airport. We spent the next several days touring England, Wales, and Scotland with Jim and his bride-to-be, Maria.

We toured some castles in Wales and Scotland and took in some kind of games in Wales, including harness racing. We also rode on a narrow-gage railroad somewhere in Wales. All in all, we had a very interesting week.

1984: Maria's folks went all-out for the wedding, including chaufered limosines. That's the only time we've ever got to ride in a Roll's Royce,. Maria's folks treated us very good while we were over there, and have visited us several times over the years. We have never been able to go back, but have many good memories. David liked it so much over there that he has gone back twice.

Sometime in this time-frame I had an interesting trip down home to Southern Arizona. Sometimes I would go down there alone and spend a few weeks visiting my family. I tried to get down there in javalina hunting season if I could, 'cause I liked to hunt them little fellers. We had our old stomping grounds to hunt in where there was no great danger of getting caught by the game warden. I was too poor to buy a non resident license.

On this particular trip we were hunting up in Abbot Canyon and hadn't had much luck. Finally I found some fresh pig tracks and had a good idea where I would find them pigs. My nieces husband was not too far away, so I went and told him what I was up to, and for him to relay this to the rest of the crew. They were hunting a couple miles down the canyon and the rig we were in was down there. I told him to have them come and pick me up at the windmill, 'cause that's where the pigs were headed.

I went ahead and caught up with the pigs, and got a couple on the ground. I gutted them out and dragged them down to the road to wait for my ride. There was some kind of miss-communication 'cause I waited till almost dark and my ride never showed up. After it got almost dark, I saw a fire start up out at the mouth of the canyon. I headed down there and when I got there Daddy was stoking that fire up and almost passed out when I walked up on him. He thought I was probably dead. The year before that I had gotten the wrong size cartridge into a rifle and damaged the gun, almost blowing it up. I put a .250-300 shell in a .243 rifle. They got to thinking I might have done something similar, or worse, this time, and was possibly laying dead or disabled. Barth, (my niece's husband) had not communicated my message to them very well.

When I got to where Daddy and Barth were, I learned that they had sent Momma to town to organize a search party to see if they could find what was left of me.

It was drizzling a little rain and we had to keep a good bonfire going. We stripped a five acre piece of ground of anything burnable before the big search party got back. We could see them down on the main road, which was a couple miles away, for close to an hour before they finally showed up. Their head-lights ran back and forth down there for about an hour before they could find the cut-off to where we were.

When they got there they had the deputy sheriff with them. Luckily it was Charlie's son-in-law, Robbie Tulk who was a deputy at that time. He took a glance at the situation and kinda figured out what was going on, and went on about his business. Some of us went up and got them pigs, and the others went home. It was quite an interesting experience, and I think the last hunting trip I ever had down there.

A comprehensive description of the next twenty years would take a lot of time, and sometimes be boring, so I will just touch on some of the peaks and valleys of that time frame.

I built a lot of fence, and did a few odds and ends in that period.

We got to watch our grandkids grow up. Glenda has four boys, and Jim has a boy and a girl. David has a two year old girl as I write this.

We spent a lot of fun times watching David excel in all the sports he played. He, in his freshman year, set a record for the Spray school that held for more than twelve years, and was only recently topped by a senior.

Daddy died in 1986, but not before he got to see and bounce on his knees his name-sake, William Martin Kennedy, who is Jim's boy. In 1987 we moved to Cove, because we knew David didn't have a snowball's chance in hell of ever graduating at Spray, because of some problems at school.

While in Cove we were able to see him do his part in leading the Cove Leopards football team back-to-back football championships, and very nearly a basketball championship. He has done well with life since he graduated, also.

We watched our oldest boy, Jim, finish a twenty year career in the Air Force and retire with honor. He has now started a new career, and is doing well.

Our daughter, Glenda, has survived adversity that would knock a lot of people off their feet. She got her college degree through all this adversity and is qualified to teach in California, where she now resides.

They have all made us very proud.

In 1989 we moved back to Spray, after we got David through school.

The saddest time of my life was in 1992, when I spent three days in the psychiatric ward of the Bend, Oregon hospital, for simply trying to make a political statement (albeit somewhat unorthodox.) When I boarded the plane for my R and R, I warned the security guard that a knife in the wrong hands could possibly be dangerous. Maybe I wasn't as crazy as everybody thought I was.

The people of Spray gave us a nice benefit party that raised $1400.00 for us that time. I would like to be able to repay that if I am ever able.

We always had music, and I have played with some very good musicians over the years. I've also done a lot of prospecting and even some hunting, over the years.

Cam lost her brother and sister in a car wreck in 1995, Her Dad died in 1997, and her Mother died in 1998. I played music for all their funerals.

My oldest brother, Charlie, died in 2000, and Momma died in 2003. I helped play music at both their funerals. Music was a big part of both of their lives.

In January of 2003, we moved here to Huntington, OR. And have gotten acquainted with many good people, including Carl and Sandy Goodwin, Mike and Beth Dolan, Earl and Bonnie Langley, and Judy Biggerstaff out toward Rye Valley, and many others here in the big city of Huntington.

We are moving on with our lives in our retirement years. I have recently reincarnated some songs that I wrote back in the early 1960's. I also wrote a condensed version of this story, and set it to music. It has been a very interesting 65 years, and I hope to see a few more before I cross that great divide. In the meantime, all we can do is "keep-a-chuggin".

                                                  Sincerely
                                                  Wilferd D. (Arizona) Kennedy
                                                  Huntington, OR. Dec. 16, 2005

My first car, A1932 Plymouth, Daddie's Model A

Our 3 kids, David, Glenda, Jim

Our 25th Wedding Anniversary, July 18, 1986

Golden Wedding Anniversary—January 3, 1983
Rear: Charlie, Clifford, Daddy, Momma, Violet, Wilferd Front:
Marjory, Peggy, Bernice, Agnes

The Huckleberry Finn Picture

*Momma's 86th Birthday—January 3, 1999
Rear: Peggy, Wilferd, Charlie, Marjory, Clifford Front:
Agnes, Momma, Bernice*

*The Kennedy Grandparents, (top) and My Parents (bottom)
are buried at the El Dorado Cemetery in the Chiricahua Mountains
My Brother, Charlie lies there, too.*

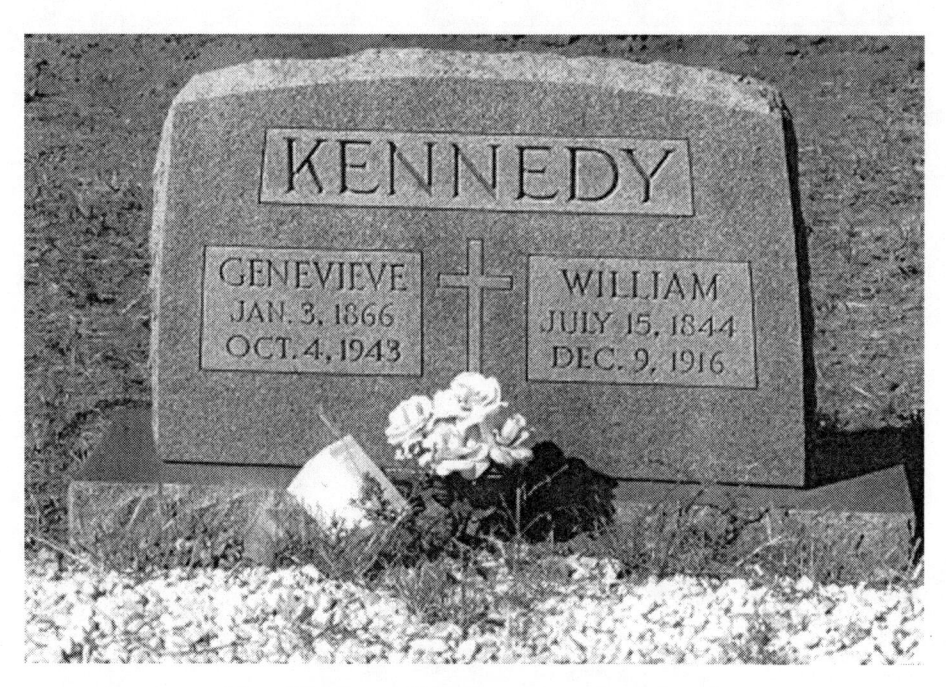

*Note: The Stoner Grandparents are buried at the
McNeal, AZ. Cemetery.*

Volume Two

Back in 1946 when I was somewhat younger than I am now, I started school in a little country school in Cochise County, Arizona, called Frontier School. It was a two room school with four grades in each room. We were just like one big happy family.

The older kids kinda looked after the younger ones and we would even play games together. That was the best school year I ever had. If I could have stayed in that little school for the next 8 years, I would have even tried to learn something. As it turned out all good things have to end. After my first grade, the county shut the school down, and started busing us to the Bisbee schools, and I never was very happy in school after that.

The teacher that taught the four upper grades in our little school (an older lady named Mrs. Martyr) had a kinda colorful past. It seems she broke one of her brothers out of jail when they were a lot younger and living over in New Mexico somewhere.

I don't know the whole story, but I guess her brother had gotten in some kind of hassle with a couple fellers and shot and killed both of them. The sheriff didn't think the killing was justifiable so they had him in jail waiting for his trial.

This young lady dressed up in men's clothes, got her a pistol, and went to the jail and convinced the jail guard that her brother didn't belong there.

I guess when he got out of there, he went to South America for about thirty years to let things cool off a little. I guess the authorities were never sure who broke him out of jail. When he slipped back into the country after his little stay in South America, he and his family moved over on Frontier Road, not too far from the old Frontier Schoolhouse.

When I was about twelve years old, I worked for one of his sons, Amos Chenowth, picking cotton. And another time about twenty years later, I helped him with his farming, after my wife and I got married, and were living with my folks down there.

I learned the story about Mrs. Martyr many years later, but thought it would be worth telling.

I guess by now you have figured out that I come from a long line of intellectuals. I think my Daddy was the smartest of the bunch. He told this story about a time when he was twelve or thirteen years old. He was already in the third grade, but was hoping someday to advance. He was at that curious age that most boys go through. He was wanting awful bad to know what the bare bottoms of them older girls in school looked like. He and a good buddy of his, Jim Hudson devised a plan.

They slipped out behind the ladies two-holer, and pried a board loose in a strategic location, and fixed them a looking place. They set back and waited for action. It wasn't too long till one of the better looking girls in school showed up to take care of business. I don't know if they drew straws or if Daddy just took pity on old Jim, but he let Jim have first go at it. Jim had just gotten his head in position for a good look when he got a full charge right square in the face. It seems like that pretty girl had a touch of diarrhea. Daddy decided not to take his turn.

Not long after that he and Jim got in some kind of mischief at school they thought might cause them a little pain, so they both jumped out an open window of the schoolhouse. Daddy spent the next seventy-six or seventy-seven years in the school of hard knocks. He was a smart man.

The old schoolhouse is still there more than ninety years later, but not being used as a school. If it could talk, it could tell a lot of good stories.

Along about the time I was twelve or thirteen years old, I had an interesting experience, not near as exciting as Daddy's, but noteworthy just the same.

A year or two before, the government had built a dam up in Rucker Canyon, creating a nice fishing lake. This was about the first year they had stocked the lake with fish.

To celebrate the occasion they decided to have a fishing derby.

We all gathered up as a family and went up there to celebrate the occasion. I doubt if any of us had a fishing pole, but it was a nice place for a picnic, anyhow.

I spent most of the day running around the hills, chasing lizards and other fairly harmless endeavors. Along in the afternoon, when they were giving out prizes to the fishermen, I heard my name called out over the loudspeaker. My first thought was to jump and run, but I got to thinking that chasing lizards wasn't a penitentiary offense, and nothing else I had done that day was too harmful, so after the third or fourth call, I hesitantly went over to see what I had done wrong.

It turned out that they were giving out prizes for the best Huckleberry Finn costume that day, and I had won, hands-down. The clothes I was wearing that day were pretty ragged, (all my clothes were) so they qualified me for the prize.

They located a big bamboo pole that I could hold to make a better picture, and sat me down with my prizes for the snap-shot. The prizes were a nice box camera and a baseball.

We still have that picture hanging on our wall, and each of our kids has the same print in their home. That was one of the few things I ever won in my life.

Along about that same time in life, I made my big singing debut. Daddy and his brother, (Uncle Cy) had played music for dances in the old Ash Creek school house, about fifteen miles north of Elfrida, for many years. They usually played about once a month.

On this particular occasion, the night had gone along pretty smooth til after midnight. We were all having a good time. Somebody in the crowd had accidentally heard me singing on the sidelines and decided I should get up on the stage with the musicians. I was (and still am) pretty bashful at the time, but finally relented. I got up and sang two or three songs, and the crowd liked it so much they were passing the hat around to pay me for my effort. I had just collected my spoils when the lights went out.

Gene Morris had furnished electricity for the dance hall for many years. He used his car battery because the electric lines had not reached that area of the valley at that time. On this night, the battery seemed to be getting a little low on power, so he and another feller were out there switching cars, so he would be able to start his at quitting time.

Andy Hamilton took exception to him dousing the lights during his favorite dance, and jumped him about it on his way back into the hall.

I'm sure Old Joe Barleycorn had a hand in what happened next, cause sober people don't act like that. Things got a little heated and old Andy, who just happened to have a whiskey bottle in his hand, took a swing at Gene with it. It missed Gene, but went on around and hit poor old Jack Brewer, an innocent bystander, right square on his cheek-bone. The blood really flew.

It took a little while to stop the bleeding some and get Jack loaded up to take him to the hospital. Things started getting serious about then. Old Gene Morris had gone and got his pistol out of his car, and they commenced to hunting for Andy Hamilton. It kinda looked like Andy"s life expectancy was pretty short at the time.

We didn't want to be any part of a killing, so we went over to Charlie's car to load up for the ride home. When we got in the car to leave, the car started rocking, and it wasn't us rocking it. Old Andy was under there. We all got back out and mingled with the crowd til things kinda cooled off and everybody went home. Then we went and helped him get out from under the car.

Old Andy lived for a good many years after that, but that was the last dance that Daddy and Uncle Ci ever played for at the Ash Creek schoolhouse. Old Joe Barleycorn has done some very serious damage in this old world over the years.

Everything I described here, I saw with my own beady little eyes.

I will take a little time here to outline a sketch of my family background. You have already seen a good part of my Daddy's background, so I will try to write some about Momma's side of the family. It will be a little sketchy, and sometimes not totally accurate, but I'll try.

Momma was born in Claremont, California, on the third day of January in 1913, the fifth child in a family of six. In 1915 the family moved to the Sulphur Springs Valley, where they homesteaded a piece of land about two miles East of McNeal, Arizona. I guess her daddy had respiratory health problems and needed a drier climate.

I guess Grandpa worked at the Douglas copper smelter while they were proving up on their homestead. In his spare time, he hand-dug a well one hundred and eighty five feet deep to get enough water for a windmill. They hauled water from one of their neighbors, a mile or two away, til he got it dug. They stayed on that homestead for several years, until Momma and one of her sisters burned their house down playing with matches.

I guess they rented a place in that area for a few years. Until they found a place on the other side of the valley on Frontier Road, that they could buy. That side of the valley had shallow water, so they jumped at the chance.

They paid good money for a homestead over there and later learned that it had not been proved up on. They were out in the cold, because Grandpa had already used up his homestead rights across the valley, and it was a one time deal.

I guess they divorced so my Grandma could homestead the place, but somebody beat them to it. She ended up homesteading an eighty acre lot a couple miles up the valley.(Three of my siblings are still living on this homestead. My oldest brother, Charlie, bought my 5 acres, and his widow, Nancy, is living there, also.)

But, I'm getting ahead of my story.

Momma and one of her sisters helped Grandma prove up on this land. They moved the old barn from the McNeal homestead across the valley to serve as Grandma's home until her death in 1947. They were required to clear five acres and make other improvements. They did this all by hand. I guess they did borrow a burro from a neighbor to do some of the farming, but most of the time Momma pulled the plow. She was a hard worker.

They started this homestead in about 1928.

Momma had a failed marriage sometime after 1930. She never talked about it much.

On her twentieth birthday, January 3, 1933, she had a marriage that lasted a little longer. That is when she married Daddy. That marriage never failed.

They spent their first winter in a make-shift tent made from an old discarded rug, and were happy as if they had good sense.

They started a family that ended in 1947, with my youngest sister, Bernice, who was number eight. I came in fifth. There were five girls and three boys, until my brother, Charlie, died in February of 2000, at age 66.

Times were tough back in the thirties, and I guess the folks had to supplement their woodcutting job by working for the W.P.A. They managed to make it through, and Daddy spent some time working at Fort Huachuca during the Second World War. He also spent some time working at the air base down by Douglas.

One day when he was working at the air base, he brought home a flight helmet all covered with blood, and a tip off an airplane propeller. It seems like some pilot had gotten too close to the airplane propeller, and had lost his head, literally. We had those articles around the place for several years.

A few years after the war was over, and all of their kids were out of diapers, Momma started working with Daddy, building houses around the valley. One year they spent the whole summer building a house over at Double Adobe and ended up not getting paid for it. That set us back pretty bad. But we kept a "chuggin"

Our good friend at the grocery store, Mr. Walker, gave us credit til we could get lined back out, and we managed to survive.

That winter, Momma was able to scrape up fifty cents to buy Christmas presents for us eight kids. She bought two twenty-five cent BB maze puzzles, and we all took turns playing with them. At least we had a good meal that day, and never complained.

All through our years of growing up, Uncle Donald, Momma's older and only brother, would bring us a sack of peanuts that he raised, some oranges and candy that he made from his honey. (he always raised honey-bees.) All three were a real treat to us. None of us was very hard to please.

The older kids in the family all pitched in as soon as they were old enough to work in the vegetable fields or the cotton patches. We all bought our own school clothes after we were about twelve years old. We made our own spending money when we were a lot younger than that. If we didn't earn it, we didn't spend it.

It was a long struggle, but we got by. We had our own shooting irons to harvest our meat. We ate a lot of cotton-tail rabbits, and we had our favorite spots where we could get a deer once in a while without getting caught. If we would have had enough water to raise a garden, we would have been in good shape. That didn't happen until I was married and Momma and Daddy were building my wife and me a house to live in.

We would need water at our new home, so I put the first real pump we had ever had (all they ever had was a windmill, before that.) in their well, and buried a line to our new home. The rest is history.

Although it was a little late to help in our younger years, it sure helped the folks in their later years. For the next thirty-five years they had the best garden in the valley. They won enough ribbons at the county and state fairs to cover a good sized quilt or two, and sold thousands of dollars worth of vegetables, besides what they gave away. Momma also grafted fruit trees and gave them away.

It would take a full-length novel to tell about all the good times we had and the good things my folks did in their many years on this old earth. There were ups and downs, but the ups have always outnumbered the downs. Monetarily, none of us has ever been too flush, but we have had something that money can't buy. As witnessed by the wonderful music and the uncontrollable laughter that can be heard at our family get-togethers that we still have once in a while.

We lost Daddy in 1986, to old age. My wife and I were not able to attend the funeral, but my brother-in-law, Dick Swisher, and a life-time friend, Raymond McCormick, collaborated to make sure we were included. Dick incorporated an audio tape of Raymond doing the eulogy with video tapes of our trip to the graveyard, and music sessions that we had on our visit down there not long after his death. We will cherish the tape forever. Daddy was almost eighty-nine.

We lost Charlie to cancer in February of 2000. We had been scheduled to play music for a dance the day he died, and we all went down and had a good dance that night. That's the way Charlie would have wanted it. Raymond

McCormick, Charlie's life-long best friend, did the eulogy at his funeral, and I was able to incorporate Taps into the song I accompanied his wife's sister on at the service. We had a nice jam session after the service. That's the way Charlie would have wanted it.

We lost Momma to old age in 2003. She was just past ninety. Raymond McCormick did the eulogy, and three of my sisters and myself did the musical at the service. Momma always loved our music so much. We went and had a nice jam session after the service.

My oldest sister, Peggy, is retired and living in a mobile home on the old home place after many years of hard work. She is seventy-one.

Brother Clifford is retired and living over at Green Valley, south of Tucson, after spending many years in the mines and the last several years of employment drilling wells in that area. He is sixty-nine.

My sister, Marjorie, at sixty-eight, is still working on a full-time job, and, with her husband, Bobby McDonald, has a pecan orchard that they operate together. It is part of Grandma Stoner's original homestead.

I guess I'm next, and I'm kinda retired, but not quite able, financially, so I'm still chasing rainbows.

Agnes is sixty-four, and she and her husband, Dick, both retired last year, she from the postal service, and he from a very successful pump business that he ran for more than thirty years.

Violet is sixty-two, and retired. She and her husband, Don Reed, are living up near Phoenix, Arizona, and doing well.

Bernice, at fifty-nine, has just retired from her job with Cochise County, She also served her time in the Navy. I think she served four years in the Navy, and twenty years in the active reserves. All and all, we've done our part in one way or another.

I'll add that Charlie's widow, Nancy, is still living in the house that we sold to them when I bought the apple orchard in 1964. But that's another story.

When Daddy turned sixty-five and retired, they deeded five acres of land to each of us eight kids. They had inherited half of the original eighty acre homestead when Grandma died in 1947.

Charlie was the one in the family that was always interested in flying. He built a lot of model airplanes, and sometimes when he was hunting, he would sit down on a rock and whittle little gliders out of the heart-wood of the mescal poles that grew down in that area. That wood is almost like balsa-wood. One day I sat and watched him make a little plane that glided more than three hundred yards on it's maiden voyage. It sure was pretty to watch. It was almost out of sight down that gentle sloping hill before it touched down.

Charlie even tried to fly on a bicycle one time. He had picked up a bicycle over in Double Adobe that had garden hoses for tires. They were wired on with baling wire, and worked pretty good in a pinch. One day he built him a ramp out of two-by-twelve boards, and I think he just piled up dirt to elevate the high end. He made a few trial runs, and was getting some pretty good distance on his jumps. So he raised the ramp a little. He went up the road (a couple hundred yards to get the maximum speed) and was on his way to a record jump. When he got about twenty feet from his ramp, giving it all he had, his head hit the ground and both wheels went straight in the air. He kept peddling for a while til he figured out that he was losing traction, and then let the bike fall on it's side. I would have had to laugh if it would have killed him, but it was more fun to watch him get up to see what had gone wrong. It turned out that one of the wires that held them garden hose tires on had broken and the hose had hooked up in the front fork of the bike. I think he benched that project til he got better tires.

Charlie was one of the calmest natured people you would ever meet. I only saw him lose his temper one time that I can remember. It was sometime after he was married and still making model airplanes. Since he liked model airplanes so well, he decided to make one for me as a Christmas gift, so I might take an interest, also. He made this nice big blue airplane (it must have had a four foot wing-span.) and gave it to me to have and to hold. He even tried to instruct me on it's maiden voyage.

He took a little while to get the motor going, as it was a little stubborn. He finally got it started, and set it down ready for take-off. It ran about twenty feet, and sputtered and died. He repeated this process three or four times with similar results. By this time he was showing signs of frustration. On the fifth or sixth try, he decided to launch it by hand. He got it started and running good and gave it a fling through the air. It flew about fifty feet, and sputtered and dived to the ground, sustaining slight damage. Charlie made a quick run to where it landed and tromped the poor old plane into a hundred pieces. That was the end of my budding aviation career.

Charlie, however, went on and graduated from model airplanes to the real thing, not too long after this incident. He bought him a little airplane and flew it for many years after that. He even made a trip or two to the big fly-in at Oshkosh, Wisconsin. And partially built an airplane, besides. He never did get it finished.

Charlie was a deadly shot with a rifle. One day he and our brother-in-law, Ronnie McDonald, were driving down the road and happened to see a coyote about four hundred yards out in the pasture. We stopped the car and

Charlie said "watch me shoot that coyote's left eye-ball out." By the time he got out of the car, the coyote was running full speed. Charlie laid the rifle barrel over the hood of the car and touched her off. That old coyote turned about three or four flips and laid still. Charlie nonchalantly blew the smoke off the gun barrel, and we went over to look at the coyote. I paced off four hundred twenty-five paces, and when we got there the coyote's left eye-ball was shot out. Ronnie and I still laugh about that every time I see him, after close to fifty years.

Charlie spent thirty years in the underground mines, mostly for Phelps Dodge Corporation. He took early retirement about 1984. After retirement, he worked part-time for our brother-in-law, Dick Swisher, on his pump rig.

He also taught himself the art of fiddle making. (He was also a pretty good fiddler.) He made more than two hundred and fifty fiddles, and hundreds of good friends before he died. He gave away almost as many fiddles as he sold, and his generosity helped many fiddlers, young and old.

About a year and a half before Charlie died, he cut the first joint off three fingers on his left hand while working on a lawn mower. He thought for a while that his fiddling days were over. It didn't hold him back for long, however.

At first he tried fiddling left-handed, but knew right away that wouldn't work. As soon as his fingers healed up enough to take the bandages off, he built him some home-made finger-tips out of wood and silicone. He would tape them on to play his fiddle. Less than a year later, he placed eleventh in a group of forty-four fiddlers in his division at the National Championship fiddle contest at Wieser, Idaho, using them home-made fingers. You can't keep a good man down. He was special.

One of his prodigies, and Arizona State fiddling champion, Jess Barry, recently abandoned a very lucrative music career to work on a ranch, and live his life more like Charlie and his wife, Nancy, had lived theirs.

On our most recent trip to visit Charlie's grave, there was a fiddle trophy beside his grave-stone that another one of his young friends had left there as a token of their love. Charlie was a good man.

When we were young some of our best times were when we went hunting. We usually went up the night before season and camped so we could get an early start on opening morning.

One time we went up the night before javalina season, and set up camp. This particular time, we happened to have a tent to stay in. When we got to our camp-site, I helped the rest of the crew to set up the tent, just like they had learned in the Boy Scouts.

There were four of us, including Clifford, my older brother, Gene and Larry Fowler, and myself.

We had just got the tent set up when the weather turned sour. It started to rain, and blew up a hurricane-like storm.

There was and old tin shed right close to our camp, where the rancher stored salt (a mineral block for the cattle) It didn't take me too long to figure out that the shed would be a drier place to spend the night than the tent. I gathered up my blankets, and moved to the shed, and invited the rest of the crew to follow suit, cause I was afraid the tent might blow down. The storm was getting stronger and stronger. They all declined my advice.

Along in the middle of the night, I was sleeping soundly in a nice dry bed, when the door busted open, and here came them other three boys, soaked to the skin, and dragging their wet soogans with them. The tent had blown down. I don't think I had enough dry bedding for the whole crew, so I think they had a miserable night. I slept like a log.

We all got up and around the next morning and went after the pigs. The weather had let up, and I think we filled our tags that day. It was a good hunting trip.

The next year we decided to hunt the same area. This time I think it was just Clifford, Daddy and myself that went. We didn't camp, but drove from home.

The night before this hunt, Clifford had found a stash of chewing gum that Momma had hidden away for special occasions. We didn't get sweets very often, so I think he took a couple pieces, cause they tasted so good. He didn't notice the big word "Feen a Mint" on the package, and it was a fairly new product at the time. So it might not have registered anyhow. He forgot to read the directions.

We drove up to where we were going to hunt, and by the time we got out of the car, Clifford was feeling a good buildup of what he thought was gas. He did what most young boys did in a case like that. He pointed his index finger at me and gave it everything he had. He filled his under drawers and both his shoes in two seconds flat, and you can bet that he read the directions before he chewed any gum after that.

I can't remember if we got any pigs that day, but I do know I had a good laugh out of it, and all and all it was a good trip.

We had a lot of good times over the years, and still do when we happen to get together.

I bought my first car when I was about twelve or thirteen. It was a 1932 Plymouth, and I bought it from Clifford for fifteen dollars. It was a good little car, and I drove it all over the back-roads in the valley. I use an Oklahoma credit card every chance I got, to acquire my running fuel.

Fuel was getting tougher to get all the time, cause people were watching closer than they used to.

One day an older friend of the family, Robert Turman, needed a ride to Elfrida. He and his cousin, Alfred Williams, had something to do. I'm not sure just what it was. I mentioned the fact that I was a little low on petrol, and they said they could fix that problem.

I guess this Cousin Alfred had been working for a widow, Mrs Slover, over near McNeal. He knew that she parked her truck where it was handy to a siphon hose.

We drove over to this old ladies place and parked my car beside her truck. While Alfred went in the house and talked to Mrs. Slover, Robert and I siphoned enough gas to last several days, directly from the truck tank into my tank. I think that was one of the rottenest tricks I was ever involved in.

Since gas was getting harder and harder to get, I tried to wean that old car over to diesel. Some of the farmers had diesel tanks that were accessible. The old thing would run on a half and half mixture of gas and diesel, but it sure did smoke. Finally the old thing gave up the ghost, and I parked it.

Sometime in the early fifties, we got our start in treasure hunting. Daddy had done a lot of prospecting in his younger days, but had gotten away from it while he was raising a family.

There was and old feller up at Elfrida, named Nelson. He had been around that area for about eighty years. He had some pretty solid information about a treasure over east of Douglas. He took my Daddy and another feller, Jimmy Wright, that was a friend of the family, over to where he thought the treasure was. They had an old military mine detector with them. I guess the old man Nelson, who was twenty to thirty years their senior, walked their legs off, as they had to walk about three miles to the treasure site. You might have guessed that they didn't find the treasure, but this trip started us on a long career as treasure hunters. I still go out treasure hunting every chance I get, more than fifty years later.

I've learned through the grapevine that someone actually did find a treasure of some consequence very near to where Old Man Nelson had taken them that day. This happened within the last ten to fifteen years.

There was a certain amount of tragedy amongst our friends and acquaintances in them days. I got to school one day when I was in the eighth grade, and all my classmates were crying. One of my better friends, Leo Cooke, had been accidentally shot and killed the night before. I guess he and his cousin were cleaning a pistol, and it accidentally discharged, hitting him in the head.

One of our bus drivers, Karl Kaiser, shot and killed his daughter, and turned the gun and killed himself, that same year, or thereabouts.

We had a good neighbor, and older man named Art Leach. He came down from his place a couple miles up the road from us, and visited quite often. Some new people had moved in next-door (about a quarter mile down the road) The last few times he came to visit us, he seemed worried that them new neighbors were out to do him harm. We didn't take him too serious, and tried to convince him not to worry. But it didn't seem to help. He finally ended up shooting himself, I guess to save his neighbors the trouble. Paranoia is not a good companion.

The kids at Lowell School, the school I attended from third through eighth grade, had a little excitement along about this time period also. The Liberty Bell, (I'm sure it was a replica) was touring the country at this time. It made a special trip into Lowell on the flat-car it was riding. We all got to go see the Liberty Bell. One of my class-mates, Sue Qualls, was picked out of the crowd to ring that bell. We were all real excited that day. I'll bet Sue never forgot it.

We had a cowboy friend that came around quite a bit in them days. He was a big feller, about six foot five inches tall, weighed about two hundred fifty. He was somewhat older than my oldest sister, Peggy, but was somewhat interested, and was also good friends with brother, Clifford. His name was Lee West. He had served some combat time in World War #2.

One night when we were all at a dance in Elfrida, Lee got too much to drink, or something, and got to seeing spooks. He backed up a short flight of stairs and had his pocket knife out. He was going to kill anyone that came close. I guess he was re-living some war experience. He had everyone in the hall buffaloed, and nobody knew what to do. Finally, my brother, Clifford, eased his way up the steps to where Lee was, and was able to talk him back to reality. It was touch and go for a while, and everyone was sure relieved when he handed Clifford his knife. It could have been disastrous.

Lee related the following story to us during one of his frequent visits to our home.

It seems like he and a couple other cowboys were camped together at a line camp on a ranch where they all worked. They would go out and work all day at whatever needed done on the ranch, then always had chores to do around camp. Lee and one of the boys pitched in and did whatever needed to be done, while this other feller went in and plopped down and read a funny-book, or something even less constructive. They let this go on for quite a while, with just a subtle hint now and then, but it bothered them some.

Finally, Lee got about all he could take and decided to do something about it. There was an open window just a few feet from where this slacker would park himself to read his funny-books. Lee grabbed his .41 Colt Revolver, pointed it out the window and pulled the trigger, at the same time jabbing that kid in the ribs with his extended thumb. I guess that as soon as the kid figured out he wasn't dead, he packed his stuff and left, and never looked back. I suspect that he might have tried to pull his own weight on his next job, who knows? I'm sure Lee has crossed the Great Divide by now, but he was an interesting character.

I well remember my first solo deer poaching trip. I was about thirteen years old. I borrowed Daddy's old model A Ford roadster to go up th Government Draw, which is about fifteen or more miles from our old home place. I got up there and parked the car down in the bottom of a big wash so it would be out of sight of the curious. I walked over the hill a half-mile or so, and got into the deer right away. I knocked down a nice fat doe. I field dressed her and dragged her back to the car and loaded her in the back. I tried to start the car, but it wouldn't start, because the battery was low on juice. I was in a bit of a pickle.

Not too long before this, we had been in a similar situation, so I knew what to do. I jacked up one of the rear wheels and blocked the others so it couldn't roll. I put the old thing in high gear and used the back wheel for a crank. It worked like a charm.

I got the old car going and headed out of the hills. I knew we had company at home, and didn't want to advertise my business, so I took the deer to the McDonald's place, which was on my way. I knew they could use some meat, and could be trusted. I got there and Mr. Ed McDonald helped me hang the deer up and skin it. By that time it was getting kinda dark, and we were having a little trouble getting it skinned. I asked Ed if it was too dark for him, and he said it was too light. He had done some real outlawing in his early years.

I ran around with the McDonald kids (mostly the twins, Pat and Mike) for many years while we were in school together. There were seven kids in their family. Their oldest brother, Bobby, married my sister, Marjory, and they're together fifty years later.

Not too long after the hunting trip I just described, Ed McDonald was riding along horseback, rolling a smoke, when his heart quit on him. I guess he was dead before he hit the ground. Not long after he died, his widow and all the younger kids moved to Oregon, so I didn't see them too often after that. I see some of the family once in a while yet. Pat, one of the twins, calls me about once a year, and we catch up on our lives as much as we can. They've been life-time friends.

Sometimes we would decide we wanted a variety of meat in our diet, so we would go up in the high Chiricahuas and get some red squirrels and turkeys, if we could find them.

One day we loaded up a big crew and headed up to the high country to see what we could come up with. There was seven or eight of us, all loaded for bear, with deer rifles and shotguns, and Charlie took his trusty little . . . 22 rifle. We got up in the end of Pine Canyon at a place called "The Sawmill." (There had been a sawmill there when Daddy was young, now there's a big church camp.) There was nothing there when this happened. A big flock (herd) of turkeys ran across the road in front of us, and we all swung into action. It sounded like a small version of World War #2 for a while, with all of us getting our share of shooting. When the smoke cleared and we went to pick up our turkeys, the only one that had anything to pick up was Charlie. None of the rest of us had touched a feather. We had a good turkey to eat, cause Charlie had made a head shot. It was a good trip.

About the only time we got any beef to eat was a few days before Christmas one year. Momma, her sister, Emma, and another husky lady (one of our neighbors) went to the mountains after Christmas trees. On their way home they saw a nice big calf standing beside the road and decided to butcher. They knew who the owner was, and he had more calves than he needed, so they shot it and loaded it on the flat-bed pickup they were driving, and covered it with Christmas trees. They drove down the road a few miles, and needed a pit-stop. When they got out and checked their load, the calf's tail was hanging out over the tail-gate. That was a close call, but the beef sure tasted good when they got it home. They never tried that again. Daddy, however, got one closer to home one time. It tasted pretty good, also.

Sometime in the mid 1950's Daddy was working with Ronnie McDonald, Peggy's husband, on a fence job up at Don Louis, a suburb of Bisbee. They dug a round, heavy piece of metal up, and brought it home. It sat around the house for a year or two and nobody paid too much attention to it. We did pick it up and tap it a few times with a piece of metal. It had a ring to it when we tapped it, and I thought it might be silver. Lead and tin and other metals make a dull sound when you tap them.

Anyhow, Charlie was molding lead bullets at this time, and ran out of lead for his bullets. He melted all but a little corner of that piece of metal that weighed about ten pounds, and made bullets out of it. Sometime later, after he had shot up most of those bullets, we took a little piece of metal that was left over, and had it assayed. It turned out to be 98% pure silver. Somebody had probably melted some silver coins. We called Charlie the Lone Ranger for a long time after that. Them were pretty expensive bullets.

One of the most interesting fellers I went to school with was Tom Hargis. He was a real quiet and nice kid, and I palled around with him some. He always said that he planned to be a veterinarian (horse doctor) when he got through school. His home-room teacher, Mrs. Woundy, encouraged him to stay with more menial work, like fence building and ditch-digging, (jobs that I later excelled at) but he didn't listen to her. He went ahead with his plans through some adversity.

I guess he had a run-in with his dad when he was a junior in high school, and had to leave home. He spent a few months living with a nice family over at Palominas, The Emery Smith family. Joe Smith was another of our good friends. Tom finished his junior year living with the Smith family, and spent his senior year living with his Grandma in Tombstone.

I guess he went on to college, and was in vet school up in Colorado when he went in the military service. He served his time in the military with the medics during the Viet-Nam war. I'm not sure how long he served over there in Viet-Nam, but while he was over there, I guess he decided to be a human doctor, instead of a horse doctor, when he came back. He went ahead and finished his schooling, and went to doctoring people instead of horses.

I hadn't seen Tom in more than forty years, but learned most of what I just related through mutual friends over the years. I also learned that he had his own clinic up in Safford, just a few blocks from the home of another good friend of mine, Leland McCormick. In fact he was one of Leland's wife, Nancy's doctors.

I stopped in at his clinic to see him one day while I was in the neighborhood. When I walked in his office, after all them years, he recognized me instantly, but it took me a while to recognize him through the weight gain and mutton-chop sideburns and mustache.

We had a nice visit and I learned that he had raised a family of four kids (all boys, I think) I think most of his kids are doctors, too, I'm not sure. He had lost his first wife to cancer, and had re-married. The thing that kind of choked me up a little was when he told me that he had had the occasion to operate on Mrs. Woundy before she died. (The teacher that more or less told him that he would never amount to much.)

I have been back to see Tom one other time and he is always glad to see me. I asked him once if he ever went back to Bisbee, and all he said was that it was too painful. I saw his daddy Tom Hargis Sr.'s obituary in the Bisbee paper a few years back, and wandered if they had ever reconciled their differences. I'll probably never know, but I know one thing, Tommy Hargis is a good man.

I wish that I could remember all the good stories that Daddy used to tell about the old times, but I can't. So I'll write down a few that I do remember.

I guess his daddy came out west not too long after he fought in the Civil War. Details are very sketchy, but sometime back in the 1870's or 1880's, Grandpa and some friends were prospecting somewhere between Silver City and Cooney, New Mexico, and were attacked by Indians. One of his partners was killed, but he and and his other buddy came through the attack alright. I'm not sure how the Indians fared.

I guess that they did find a pretty good gold deposit and worked it for a while. But it didn't make him rich. Along in the early 1880's, I understand that Grandpa was working in El Paso, Texas, for the railroad. About this time he must have gotten married, because Daddy's oldest sister, Carmen, was born in 1882 or 1883. They must have homesteaded in Southeastern Arizona around that same time-frame, because my Aunt Carmen supposedly could recall going through the big earthquake that hit that area in 1887. I think they moved from El Paso to their homestead in some kind of a wagon. They ended up having fourteen kids, nine of which survived to maturity. Daddy was number six of the survivors.

Sometime while Grandpa was working on the railroad, he and another feller were able to requisition a couple o silver bars. Some mining company had a big shipment of silver on the train, and he and his buddy knew they didn't need all of it. So while they were stopped at a siding, Grandpa and this feller borrowed a couple bars and buried them in the bushes beside the track. Unless the other feller went back and dug it up, (which isn't likely) that silver is still where they buried it. Grandpa told Daddy where it was, before he died, and Daddy told our family where it is, but we've never gotten around to really looking for it. Maybe someday I will go take a look. It would sure be worth finding.

Daddy's folks raised turkeys when he was a little feller, and he had the job of herding them turkeys. There were a couple of mean bulls in one pasture where he ran them turkeys, and they would run him up a tree every now and then. He sure hated them bulls.

A few years before that, a feller was digging a well in that pasture, and the bottom fell out. I guess he got out all right, but they never did find the bottom of that well. They ran more than a quarter mile of wire down that hole and couldn't find the bottom.

One day Daddy happened to be in that area with his turkeys. He watched them two bulls fighting over close to that well. I guess he was one of the happiest boys alive when he saw them two bulls disappear down that well. He didn't have to worry about being treed by them two bulls anymore. I don't know if he ever told the owner of those bulls, or not.

When he was about eight years old, Daddy and his brother, Cicero, would sometimes ride burros twenty-five miles to play music for dances. I guess they would grab their instruments and get an early start to their destination, then play all night, and ride back home the next day. Any money they collected when people passed the hat to pay the musicians, was given to Grandpa when they got home. NO wonder Daddy left home when he was twelve or thirteen.

After he left home, Daddy went to work for one of the most honest people in Cochise County at the time. One day about sundown, this honest man came a chasing a big slick-ear (unbranded) calf into the barn lot. He wanted to get it in the barn out of sight as quick as possible, so it's momma wouldn't find it before it was well weaned. When they got up the next morning, one of his own cows was standing out there bawling for her calf. He had stolen his own calf. That's the way it was in them days. And I'm not sure it has changed much since.

Another thing happened before Daddy left home thats worth mention.

One of the ranchers in that area, named Luther Price, had put his ranch up for sale this one year. I guess several prospective buyers had come up missing. One day when Daddy and Grandpa were on their way home from selling a big wagon-load of turkeys in Willcox (which was a two day trip each way.) this Luther Price feller came out of nowhere, and decided to ride along with them. I guess they were probably pretty lucky that they were able to make camp in the little community of Lite that night. There's safety in numbers.

Not long after their trip to Willcox, they learned that old Luther had gotten caught trying to kill his sixth ranch buyer. I guess he would take them buyers out to show them around the ranch, and knock them in the head when they least expected it, take their money and throw them in an old well that was handy. He killed five buyers before he got caught, and I'm sure Daddy and Grandpa were possible victims if they hadn't camped near other people.

Along about that same time, Daddy and his oldest brother, Dave, were camped in a little cabin somewhere around that area. Along about dark a big old cat tried to get in their cabin with them. I guess it smelled the meat they had, and it must have been real hungry. They must have left their guns at home that time, cause they didn't shoot it. It tried for quite a while to get in that old cabin, then finally gave up. They were sure scared.

When morning finally came, they went and found help and they tracked that cat down and killed it. It was a big old jaguar that measured eleven feet from the nose to the tip of his tail. I guess whoever got it had a full-mount made of that cat, and donated it to the University of Arizona, where it stayed for a good many years. It may still be there, I don't know. That happened about ninety years ago.

Daddy and a couple of his brothers kicked around the country, working in several different mines from Globe, Arizona, to Silver City, New Mexico. They played a lot of music everywhere they went. Daddy played the guitar, and had at least three brothers that played the fiddle. They made good music.

About 1918, Daddy and his brother, Frank, who was quite a lot older, almost had a run-in with the Sheriff of Cochise County, an ex-Arizona Ranger, Harry Wheeler. He was nobody to fool with, I guess.

Daddy and brother Frank were hauling a piano or some other heavy piece of furniture from Gleeson to Courtland for somebody. They got bogged down and stuck in the middle of the road, blocking the road. When Sheriff Wheeler came along in a hurry, and couldn't get by, he was ready to shoot both of them for blocking the road. I'm not sure just how they resolved the problem, but I guess they were a little worried for a while. I guess the feller that was with Wheeler kinda calmed him down, and maybe they helped get the rig unstuck. Daddy never did say, but he said that old Harry Wheeler was a pretty rough character. He had killed several men when he was an Arizona Ranger.

Daddy and his brother Cicero (Uncle Cy to us) started a restaurant business in Courtland along about that same time. I guess Courtland, Gleeson, and Pearce were all booming towns at that time. I guess Uncle Cy's wife, Mamie, ran the business for them while the men worked in the mines. Daddy said that they had a pretty good business going, and might have gotten rich, if all their hungry kinfolks hadn't found their place. There were too many free-loaders, and their business didn't last too long.

One night while they were living in that area, there was a shoot-out over in Gleeson. One feller was killed outright, and the other high-tailed it out of there on horseback. They didn't bother to follow the old boy that night, but the deputy in Gleeson decided to go after him the next morning. Daddy and Uncle Cy happened to be there that morning (they probably had played for a dance the night before.) The deputy kinda deputized the two of them, and they jumped in his rig to go after the killer.

They hadn't gone more than two or three miles when they must have seen the fellers horse. I guess they got out of the rig and went on foot for a ways. They saw the old boy sitting leaned up against a yucca plant. The deputy tried to call him out, but he didn't seem to want to move. They circled around behind him and sneaked up on him. When they got to where he was at, rigor mortis had set in pretty good. The feller he killed had got his licks in, too. They loaded his body up and took it back to town, and the case was solved.

Daddy went to New Mexico sometime in the 1920's, but I'm not sure just when or why. He did say that he went and found the place where his Daddy had mined gold back in the 1870's. He talked a lot about prospecting around Pinos Altos with a good friend named Ramon Campos. I guess they were able to make beans with their gold pans in that area. He said you could see little nuggets rolling down some of those little washes during a good rain-storm, and once in a while they would pick up a pretty good nugget. Sure sounded like fun to me.

Daddy also mentioned something about a haunted house he lived in in Silver city. It seems like the people that owned the house had been scared out by a ghost of some kind. They just let him stay there for free, if he could get along with the ghost. The ghost was just a big pack-rat up in the ceiling of the house. When he got rid of it, he had a ghost-free, rent-free home for a quite a while. I think he might have even bought the place, I'm not sure. He did buy some property in Silver City, I know. He showed it to me when we went there on a trip many years later.

He also talked about working in a manganese mine a few miles south of Silver City for a year or two. Prohibition was still in force, but he had a source for some rot-gut whiskey, which he shared with his boss, Mr. Kirchman. They got along pretty good after that. He also talked about a big sheet of solid native silver that he found down in one of the tunnels he did some work in. He told the boss about it, but silver wasn't worth much at the time, so he didn't do anything about it.

Daddy also talked about a car wreck he was in that could have been fatal. He turned over a Model T Ford, and was pinned to the ground with the gear shift lever poked through his gut. A feller by the name of Johnny Redlinger single-handedly lifted that car off of him and got him to the hospital where they could fix him up. I'm sure that saved his life. He came back to Arizona not too long after that happened.

During the Second World War, when Daddy was working over at Fort Huachuca, he sometimes imbibed a little on Friday night before he came home from work. One night he was in this condition and driving a little too fast to suit the Highway Patrolman, Mr. Holly. The cop pulled him over and was standing by his car window, talking to him, when the brave-juice kicked in. He figured he could slap that officer and knock him out long enough to get away. He slapped the old boy with everything he had. The officer just shook his head, and grabbed Daddy and dragged him out of the car. He said "you're a tough little S O B, aren't you?" But didn't abbreviate. He took him to the courthouse, and I guess they took his drivers license away and fined him a hundred and fifty dollars. I don't think he ever got his drivers license back, and I'm sure he was never able to pay the fine. They would have kept him in jail for a while, but they didn't want to feed six or eight Kennedys. Most of the time we were growing up, Momma did most of the driving.

Daddy did drive some in his later years. He did a lot of bottle hunting. When I was down in that country, he and I would go all over the country, digging up old garbage dumps for their antique bottles. Sometimes the whole family would go with us. One day we took a trip up to the foothills of the Chiricahua Mountains, to the old Kennedy home-place where Daddy was raised. I found an old whiskey bottle and some other stuff that I kept for years. We had a good trip that day. Daddy and I spent a lot of good times running around the country down there. We went to all the ghost towns from Steins Pass, New Mexico, to Pearce, Arizona, and places in between. Daddy sold some of the bottles we found, and gave a lot of them away.

When I was not around, Daddy would go out on his own, and hit all the ghost towns from Gleeson to Pearce. One day he was waving to some friends he made along the way, and ended up in the ditch with the car on its side. They were able to help him get it upright and out of the ditch, and the damage was minimal.

Another time, he was showing two couples from England around the old mine dumps at Courtland, not far from where he had wrecked, when a feller with a shotgun in his hand, and wearing a ski mask, walked out to where they were and told them they were trespassing. When they got back to their rigs, he had followed them. He pointed his shotgun at them and demanded all their valuables. I guess one of the Englishmen tried to wrestle the shotgun away from the feller, and while they were scuffling, Daddy threw his wallet under his car. The feller was too tough for the Englishman, and went ahead and took all their cameras and money. But when it came Daddy's turn, all he had was less than a dollar in change, and the feller never even took it. He had about a hundred dollars in his wallet that was under the car.

They went and called the law after the feller left, but it didn't do much good. Daddy described everything about the whole deal, including the rig the robber was driving, to no avail. Daddy always thought that the feller was somehow involved with the lawmen, because they tried to confuse Daddy when he described everything. Daddy thought he knew who the robber was, but the law never did go after him. Daddy thought the robber was one of their rancher friends, and there is a good chance that he was sharing his spoils with them. I'll bet them Englishmen had a story to tell when they got back to England.

It wasn't too long after this incident that Daddy had to quit driving for good. He would usually stop at the local watering hole in Gleeson for a little liquid refreshment before he headed home at night. It was about twenty-five miles from home and he had to go through Elfrida. One night he was running a little late, and Momma got worried and went looking for him. She found him still sitting at the bar, and told him she thought it was time to go home. I guess it upset him some, so he jumped in his car, and straddled the center line, driving as fast as he could, till the law stopped him about halfway home. I don't know how many cars he had run off the road, but I'm sure there were quite a few. The ditches in the area are not very steep, so he didn't cause any wrecks, but the law was not too happy, nonetheless. Considering he hadn't had a driver's license since 1942, and this happened in the early eighty's, I think he got off pretty easy. The cop that caught him told him if he promised never to drive on the highway again, he wouldn't take him to jail or give him a ticket. As near as I know, that is a promise he kept till the day he died. Momma picked him up in her car that night, and somebody went and got his car the next day. They say all good things have to end.

Daddy met some nice people while he was prowling around the area. There were some javelina hunters from over by Yuma that he showed where to find the pigs. They were forever grateful. They always brought Daddy a gift when they came over hunting. One time they brought him a bottle of champaign. The next morning we heard a loud bang and heard Daddy let out a howl. When we got to the kitchen where he was, his right eye was red and watering. He had popped the cork on the champaign, and it had hit him in the eye. I guess he just didn't understand the high-toned things in life. Not long after that Daddy and I made our last outing together. We went up to our mining claims east of Gleeson. We bumped into the Yuma boys, had a nice visit, and spent a few hours just relaxing. I had to come back to Oregon a few days later. A few days after that Daddy got sick and never did get back on his feet. He passed away about nine months later.

In the spring of 1962 I went to work in the underground mines in Bisbee, and spent a year as a mucker. It was a good experience, and I made enough money to pay cash for two homes in that year. I also had several close calls down there. There are a lot of visible dangers, and some that you can't see.

One time one of the miners I worked with took my place in the "happy hunting ground", as I described in my first volume. Another time I was working with a timber man named Louie Garcia in the drift (tunnel). If I had listened to him, this story would have been a lot shorter. We were cleaning up a spill (where rock had worked loose and was falling in the tunnel), and it looked a little dangerous to me. I told Louie it might be a good idea to bar down the material that was hanging above our heads. He poked it a couple times with the bar, and said he thought it was all-right. He went ahead and got under the dangerous looking rock and picked some material loose so I could muck it into the ore car. I still didn't trust that ceiling, so instead of getting under the bad spot behind the ore car, I got in beside the car, and threw the muck over my shoulder. About the third shovel full, I had close to a ton of boulders in my muck stick (shovel). The boulders fell where I would have been standing if I had listened to that Mexican. Louie sure had a startled look on his face, but we both lived through it. That was too close for comfort. There were two or three other incidents that made me choose a different vocation. When my year was up, I came back to Oregon.

I met a lot of good people in my year in the mines, and don't regret it for a minute. One feller I worked with was the first dowser I ever ran into. He claimed he could find gold and other good things with a little bobber he had made out of a little wooden tube hung on a key chain. We had two or three interesting trips together. We didn't find anything that was valuable, but it is always fun being out in the hills trying. His wife showed my wife how to make enchiladas, and that has been an old stand-by with our family ever since. I don't know if he ever found anything worth finding, and can't even remember his last name, but Jim was a nice feller to prowl the hills with.

It seems like that was the same year that Daddy and I decided to go over to Silver City and check out some of his past experiences. We mainly wanted to see if we could get down in that old mine where he had found that big plate of silver when he was a young feller.

We got over there and found the old mine was closed down and had filled up with water. He showed me where the miners had dumped their spent carbide from their lamps when they came off shift, and several other features of the old mine that he remembered, including the approximate area where the silver had been. There was a hundred feet of water on top of it by then.

We went on to Pinos Altos and panned a little gold, and looked the place over pretty good. Daddy had found what he thought could have been an old

Spanish mine up there when he had been there in the early days. He said that he had found a fence post that just floated in the post-hole. The ground sounded hollow when he stomped on it. We were not able to find the right place, but it was an interesting story.

I think we spent the night at Pinos Altos, and fooled around for a while the next day. Then came back to Silver City where he showed me the property that he had owned. We were able to locate Johnny Redlinger, the feller that had saved his life so many years before. They had a nice visit, and we learned that Daddy's old boss, Mr. Kirchman, was living in Lordsburg, New Mexico, which was on our way home. So we headed for Lordsburg.

It was late when we got to Lordsburg, so we went out of town a mile or two, and rolled out our bedroll and bedded down. Along in the middle of the night we woke up to some big black animal sniffing our heads. I spooked us for a few seconds, till we saw that it was some black Angus cows that were just curious. When we got up in the morning, we found that Mr Kirchman was out of town, but got his address, so that Daddy could contact him later. They got together after I came back to Oregon, and worked together for several years on some mining claims that had been given to us by an old friend of the family. We held them claims for about thirty years, until the mining laws changed, and we were not able to hold them anymore.

After we went back to Oregon in 1963, Momma and Daddy and Bernice came through Mitchell, where we were living, on their way to Alaska. We went with them to Seattle, where they caught the plane to Anchorage. Some nice black man offered to carry their luggage, and they went ahead and let him. When he was done and reached his hand out for a gratuity, Daddy shook his hand and thanked him, and went on about his business. We hadn't needed his help, anyhow, but he sure had a puzzled look on his face when we saw him last. We took their car back to Mitchell, and went back and picked them up in the fall when they came back down.

They had a real good time in Alaska that summer. They picked and sold a lot of wild berries, and drove all over the few existing roads in Alaska, driving a rig they had borrowed while they were up there.

The next time they went to Alaska was in 1965, with Dick and Agnes. We were living in Union, Oregon, on our apple orchard. Dick and Agnes and Daddy drove on up the Al-Can Highway. Momma stayed with us for a couple months to help us when our new baby girl, Glenda, was born. We put her on the bus in La Grande, to go to Portland and fly up to Anchorage, when the baby was a week or two old. They had another good summer up in Alaska, and when it came time to go South for the winter, they drove down the Al-Can Highway in an old International pickup that had been given to them by Bobby McDonald. They had to park the old pickup on a hill every day when they camped for the night, because the battery wouldn't hold a charge. When they got to our place in Union, about three thousand miles from Anchorage, they found that one of the cells in the battery had a hole in it, and all the acid had leaked out.

They spent a month or more at our place in Union and helped remodel a house that was on it. We were living in a single-wide trailer till we got the house fixed up.

While they were there, elk season opened, and Daddy and I did a little elk hunting. One day when we were up there hunting, we were driving down the road, and saw some tracks that looked fresh. We got out of the pickup and took a short walk up the hill to see if we could tell which way the elk had gone. I know we were no more than two hundred yards from the rig when we got back together to go back. We started back in the direction we thought would take us back, and walked close to a mile before we figured out we were lost. Finally we found an old abandoned road, that we knew would take us back to the road we were parked on, sooner or later. It turned out to be about three miles later.

When we finally came out on a road that was being used, we bumped into another hunter, and figured we were back in business. We asked the hunter where we were, and he said he didn't know, cause he was lost, too. Back to the drawing board we went. We took off down the road, and hadn't gone too far when I recognized a camp we had passed on our way in that morning. The road made a big circle, and we were on the wrong side of the circle. As near as I could figure, we were about six miles from our rig, by road. so we started out toward the pickup. We finally caught a ride about two thirds of the way back to the rig, but had still had a long hike that day. We didn't find any elk, but we sure slept good that night. It was a good trip, in spite of our getting lost. That was the last trip Momma and Daddy ever made to Oregon or Alaska, and I think they really enjoyed it. They had a lot to talk about for a long time after that.

Along in the early 1970's, an old feller named Mayfield, up in Gleeson, showed Daddy and Dick Swisher a double handful of gold coins. He said these were his share of a treasure he and two other fellers had dug up over east of Douglas. He said the coins had been in a saddle bag, and they had never found the second saddle bag. (saddle bags come in pairs) He told them the area where they had found it, and described the location pretty good.

We decided that with any luck we could go over there and find that other saddle bag with our metal detectors. We made several trips over there and covered a lot of ground, but couldn't find the place that he had described. We did find some good fire agate, and other good polishing rock, however. We brought some home each trip.

About 1975 or 1976, I learned that Eddie McDonald, and another feller named Ralph, had a rock shop over in Sisters, Oregon. I thought it would be a good idea to go down and bring back some of the fire agate to sell at their shop. Eddie and I struck out and went down to get some of the fire agate.

We spent several days over there and gathered up a good quantity of agate. I'm sure there was at least a couple hundred pounds of high-grade, and three or four hundred pounds of lower grade agate. I know we had at least ten thousand dollars worth of rock all together.

Eddie and I loaded all we could get in my little V.W. Bug, and left the rest for his brother, Mike, to bring up in his pickup in a few days. We thought we were probably set for life.

Eddie acted a little strange all the way back to Oregon. When we got back to Sisters, I should have realized why, when Ralph came out of the house buttoning his pants up. I didn't know their sleeping arrangements, so the silence didn't register on my thick head.

I unloaded all the fire agate we had and went on home to Mitchell. I never heard a thing from over there for a few weeks, until I went to a rock show in Prineville. Ralph was there, and his face was still scarred up pretty good. I guess Eddie had worked him over plenty good the day we got back from Arizona. He had just jumped out of Eddie's wife's bed. I'm sure that ended their partnership. I learned this later through the grapevine.

I went back to get some of my fire agate a week or two later, and five hundred pounds of good rock had disappeared for good. I ended up bringing about twenty pounds of low-grade rock home, and Ralph had stolen the rest.

When I got back to Mitchell with the little bit of rock I had salvaged, I ran into a feller that claimed to be one of the best fire agate grinders in the country. I let him have what little rock I had left, and let him use a little shop I had on one of my rentals in town. He was to grind and polish the rock on shares. He fiddle-farted around for several weeks, and had a small handful of the stones partially worked up. He borrowed an old V.W. Van that I had, to live in while he promoted our agate. He ended up over in Sisters, and after a few months, I finally went over and got the V.W. Van, and let him have the rest of the fire agate. I ended up with one small stone that another couple (that I met a couple years later), finished and set in a ring for us. That's not a very impressive ten thousand dollar ring, but I guess the experience was worth something. I've had other ventures that ended up worse. Life goes on.

The folks had a lot of good trip looking for buried treasure over the years. I missed out on most of the trips, since I was living and raising a family in Oregon. I didn't get to spend much time down in Arizona. Once in a while I would get in on one of their trips.

Not too long after we moved to Spray, Oregon, in 1978, I made the acquaintance of the second big-time dowser I had met. And old feller named Glenn Peck lived in Spray at that time, and he claimed he could run a pencil point, or similar object, around on a map, and locate a treasure on that map. We had been hunting the big Skeleton Canyon treasure for twenty-five or thirty years at that time, so I got him a map of the area where we had been hunting. He ran a pencil around the map, and put a big x where he thought it would be. He also made me a dowsing rod to take to Arizona, and find the treasure. My sister, Marjorie, is a well dowser, and we figured she could dowse for gold, also.

When I got down there that winter, we gathered up a big crew, and went up to where the old man had marked the big x on the map. We all got out, with Marjie in the lead with the dowsing rod, pointing the way.

That little rod was doing just as it was supposed to do. We hadn't gone too far when we found a big rock that we thought must be the treasure marker. Sure enough, when we paced off the right distance, that little rod said the treasure was there. We had our digging tools with us, and it didn't take long to dig a hole six or eight feet deep. We all took turns digging, and I think Daddy, who was only about eighty years at the time, dug more than any of us. We kept checking with a metal detector as we went down, but never did come up with a signal of any kind. Finally, we decided that it was a false alarm, and covered up the hole, and went back to the drawing board. We've had other similar trips over the years, and have always come up empty. But it sure is fun trying. I've met quite a few dowsers over the years, but I haven't met any rich dowsers.

When we were kids growing up, we had an old feller for a neighbor, named Mr. Saarick. He would sometimes come down and play the fiddle. He had a Stradivarius fiddle and drove an old Dodge car (1926-1929) His boy, Henry, had a 1913 Model T Ford that he drove. All of these items burned up when their garage burned sometime in the 1950's.

Neither of his boys had ever married or produced any offspring that he knew about, so when he was getting along in his eighty's, he decided he wanted some grandkids. He figured his boy, Henry, who was only about sixty-five or so could probably still produce.

One day he came down and put the proposition up to Daddy. In his German accent (he was from the "old Country") he said to Daddy "You have a daughter, and I have a son, and I need some grandkids. I have lots of money to go with the project" My youngest sister, Bernice, who was seventeen or eighteen at the time, was the daughter he was talking about. Daddy didn't think it was a real good proposition, so he refused the offer. We got a good laugh out of it, anyhow.

My oldest brother, Charlie was working in the mines in Bisbee at the time, and for many years thereafter. Since the old man Saarick's car had burned, and he was getting old and blind, Charlie would take the old feller to town once or twice a month to pick up groceries and stuff. The old feller always carried his lunch box with him, and wouldn't let it out of his sight. This went on for several years, until the old feller died at age ninety-four. When they looked in his lunch box to see what was in it, there was more than thirty thousand dollars in it. He was quite an old character.

Charlie had his favorite fishing place up in Cave Creek Canyon. We made several trips up there over the years. I remember one time when my son, Jim, was about twelve or thirteen, Jim and I went up there with Charlie. We caught a nice string of fish, and were on our way out, when I decided to show Jim how to run down a steep hill. I got to running off that steep hill, and was doing pretty good till my toe hooked under a root. My feet went straight up in the air, and I turned a flip in the air before I landed on my shoulders and the backpack I was packing. I could see the startled looks on Jim and Charlie's faces as I was on my way down, and upside down. It didn't hurt me any at all, but I didn't try running any more after that. We had a good trip.

One other time, we went up to the White Mountains with Charlie and Daddy. Charlie was building an airplane, and had learned where an airplane had crashed, where he could get some parts for his airplane. We went up there, and while Charlie and Daddy were working on the airplane, Jim and I borrowed a fishing pole. We went on down the hill to a creek that was just full of pan-sized trout. We took turns with the pole, and caught twenty or thirty trout in a half hour or so. We went back up with our trout and helped pack the airplane parts out. That was another good trip. Charlie never did finish building his airplane, but I think he had fun working on it.

The last trip we made to Cave Creek, David went with Charlie and me. We got up there and Charlie demonstrated how to catch fish, while David and I watched. There was several inches of snow on the ground, and it was pretty cool up in the canyon. When we got to the bottom of the waterfall, Charlie had a frying pan and some flour and grease and salt and pepper stashed. We were all set for a fish fry. We got a fire started, and while I was cleaning the fish, Charlie was dipping them in the flour and putting them in the hot grease. One of the fish took off swimming in the skillet and almost jumped out. That was about the freshest fish we've ever had to eat. It was a fun trip, and we'll always remember it.

I always had a lot of fun hunting javelinas, if I was down in that country when the season was on. I would help fill the tags of the family members that had tags. We had places where we were pretty safe from the law.

One year. Jim happened to be down there when the season opened, so he got to take his turn with the pigs. We went to one of our favorite spots, and took off hunting. We hadn't gone very far when I spotted some pigs a half a mile or so up the dry wash where we were. The wind was blowing from the pigs to us, so we had an easy stalk. We just walked up the bottom of the dry wash till we were about where I thought the pigs should be. We peaked over the bank, and they were about fifty yards away. I let Jim pick out the pig he wanted, and he knocked it down with one shot. I think we might have gotten two pigs that day, but I'm not sure. As always, it was a good hunt. We always had a lot of fun, and I kinda miss them good times.

In the early to mid 1970's, I spent a few elk hunting seasons hunting with Joe and Fred Fitzgerald, and some other fellers over on Heppner Mountain. We would usually camp for several days over there and give them elk a run for their money.

One of the first elk we got when I was with them, was a nice spike bull. We had made a short hunt, and I was on my way back to the rig, when this little bull ran out of the brush about half-way between me and the other fellers. They were standing at the rig. As soon as it was safe for us to start shooting, the bullets really flew. I got off one shot that I knew had missed, but three of the other fellers emptied their guns at that poor old bull. Each one of them knew they had hit that bull at least twice, so all we had to do was track him down, and we had our elk. We took out after that bull and hadn't gone too far till we heard a single shot. We knew somebody else had gotten our crippled bull. We went ahead and followed the tracks for a couple hundred yards, and sure enough, somebody had killed the bull. Luckily, it happened to be Fred Fitzgerald, who had come over from Mitchell that day without our knowing.

We went ahead and helped butcher the bull. When we got it skinned out, we found one bullet hole in that animal. Nobody had touched a hair, but Fred. We all had a good laugh over the whole deal afterwards.

Another time, Joe and Fred had other commitments for the opening day of season, so I went over and met the two fellers from Bend, Oregon, that hunted with us. They were Claude and Gary Ward, a father and son that we had gotten acquainted with a year or two before.

On opening morning, I had them let me off a mile or two from our favorite elk crossing. They went ahead and waited for me to hunt through to them. I was not far from where they were waiting, when I jumped two spike bulls. I shot one of them and the other went over to where Gary was at, and he shot it. We spent most of the day that day, taking care of them two bulls.

We had a light snowstorm that night and the next morning I hit a fresh bull track right off the bat. I hadn't followed him too far when he jumped up, and I got a bullet in him. I followed the blood trail for about a half mile, and finished him off. By the time we got my four-point bull back to camp, Fred and Joe showed up to help hang it up and skin it. I can't remember for sure if we killed any more elk that season, or not, but you can bet we had a good time trying.

One of the last times I hunted with Fred and Joe, we spent about eight or nine days chasing them elk, and came up empty. We had one day of season left, but everyone had to go home, except Fred and me. We spent the night and had a good blanket of fresh tracking snow the next morning.

We got in the rig to go down to our favorite area, and hadn't gone far when we found some fresh elk tracks. I let Fred out to track that bunch of elk. I went on down the road a short distance, and hit a good bull track. I followed that bull a couple of miles, and jumped a big cow. I went ahead and shot her, because Fred had a cow tag. I gutted the cow, and propped her open so she would cool out, and went back and followed my hunch, that the elk I killed was not the one I had been tracking. I could tell by the tracks that it was a bull. Sure enough, I hadn't gone far when I picked up his track, and followed him till I jumped him and killed him. He was a nice five-point bull. I gutted him out and went looking for Fred. When I found him, he had blood on his hands, so I knew right off we had more elk than we had tags for.

There was another feller there from another camp, and he offered to help drag my bull out when I told them I had one down. We had to drive three or four miles to get close to my bull. When we got there and were walking up the hill to drag him out, I got a chance to ask Fred how many elk he had down. He indicated that he had two down. We didn't broadcast the fact to our helper, and went on back and loaded up one of Fred's cows, and headed for home with two elk.

When we got to Joe's place, we called Gary back from over at Bend, and when he got back with the other cow tag, we went back over and got the other two elk in the middle of the night. It was three or four o'clock in the morning when we got them elk all skinned out. That was a good hunt. Fred and I talked about it when I went to see him in the hospital a week or two before he died. We had a lot of good times together. I still think of Fred some thirty years after his death.

In 1970, I went to Alaska to build guardrail for Mount McKinley Fence Co. When we were working over on the Canadian border, we met an interesting couple that lived out there. I guess they had homesteaded their place. They lived in a little log cabin they had built. The old man was a retired navy captain, and his wife was a pretty good artist, specializing in Alaska scenes. I commissioned her to paint a nice picture of Alaska landscape, with a group of moose in the foreground. We've enjoyed that painting for a good long time.

I also spent a month or more up in Nome, where I was to meet and visit with some of the Eskimo people. They were quite interesting to visit with.

Towards the end of the summer, I was working out of Fairbanks, and the boss sent me down to Healy, about a hundred miles Southwest of Fairbanks, to remove some guardrail so they could widen the road. The last morning I was there, I was sitting across the table from one of the construction workers eating breakfast, and got to talking. In the course of our conversation, I mentioned that I was working for Mt. McKinley Fence Co. He asked me if I knew a feller by the name of Bobby McDonald that had worked for the company at one time. Bobby just happened to be married to my sister, Marjorie, and when he mentioned Bobby, I recognized him. I hadn't seen him in more than eighteen years. When I was twelve years old I had worked for him on a ranch he was running down in Double Adobe, Arizona. He was Bobby's uncle, Mutt Shortes, and I had worked herding cows out of a cotton patch for the ranch he was running. My job was to keep the cows out of the cotton till the pickers got all the cotton picked. After the cotton was picked, the cows were turned in the field to clean up the cotton that was left. Cows do pretty good on cotton stubble. The cotton seed has a lot of nutrition in it.

Anyhow, we had a nice visit, (Mutt and I) that day, and I haven't seen him since, but it sure goes to show you what a small world we live in.

When I worked in Valdez, Alaska in 1975, I ran into another feller that had been raised in Double Adobe, Arizona. He had been a good friend of my oldest brother, Charlie. He had flown back from Arizona with Dick Swisher, and they had somehow learned each others business or capacity in the scheme of things in Valdez. George Dalton was this feller's name, and he was some kind of foreman for Morrison and Knutson (M.K.) on the pipeline terminal where we were building a security fence. He had learned that Dick was married to a Kennedy from down in Southeastern Arizona, and when I met him the first thing he asked was "Which Kennedy are you?" I saw him a few times while we worked up there, and learned that he was living in Cottonwood, Arizona at that time, but haven't seen him since. Like I say, it's a small world.

When we went to England in 1984, I had another experience with a small world. We had a very nice vacation over there, and on about the last day of our trip, we went to London to see the sights. We caught a bus out of Wheatly, where we were staying with our new daughter-in-law's folks, (Robert and Marguerite Horwood). When we got to London, we were going to use the subway to get around the city. The first time we got on the subway train, I got to visiting with some people and learned they were from Bend, Oregon, just a hundred miles from Spray, Oregon, where we lived at the time. I got so involved talking that when the train stopped at a station, and all the rest of my family got off the train, I was still talking. When I realized the train didn't wait around for stragglers, we were already on our way. I tried to tear the door open as I was watching my family disappear before my eyes, and knew I was lost for good in downtown London.

I guess Jim got a little excited when I disappeared on that train, and when Maria told him that anyone with a lick of sense would know to get off at the next station and catch the next train back, he knew I was gone for good. As it turned out, the people from Oregon that I was talking to, suggested to me that I should do just that. Everybody seemed pretty happy to see me when I came back on the next train, and you can bet I was the first one in line when we got off the train after that.

We went ahead and toured London that day. We went to Trafalgar Square, where they feed the pigeons, and then to Buckingham Palace. When we got to Buckingham Palace, there was a small crowd gathering, so we thought maybe we were going to see the changing of the guard. We waited a few minutes and a big motor-caide came around the bend of the road leading to the palace. President Reagan and his wife, Nancy, were in one of their limousines, on their way to see the Queen. They waved as they went by, and we walked on over to #10 Downing Street. We hadn't been there very long, when Margaret Thatcher came out of her home and got in her limo, to go visit with President Reagan at Buckingham Palace, I guess. She waved at us as they drove by on their way out. I suspect that I was probably the only person in London that day that was wearing a cowboy hat. We had a very interesting day, and got to see everybody but the Queen.

We, as a family, owned several mining claims for more than thirty years, from the early 1960's, till 1993, when the government changed the mining laws to make it harder on the small scale miners. I had several claims besides the ones owned by the family members.

We were able to lease the family claims out a couple of times, but were never able to get any production on them. We did receive some advance royalties, so it wasn't a total loss when we had to let them go. Since we let the claims go back in 1993, I have filed on other claims, some of which I still own.

I had a single claim over on Desolation Creek, between Long Creek and Ukiah, Oregon, for several years. The previous owners of the claim had indicated that there was some high-grade gold ore on the property, so I thought it would be a good project for my brother, Clifford, and Me. I went and bought a homemade core drill from a feller in La Grande, Oregon, and called old Clifford up to see if he would help to drill some test holes on the property. He was game, and came up from Southern Arizona to help with the drilling. He spent a week or ten days up there drilling, and we took our ore samples to a local assayer, named Chuck Chase, in Baker, Oregon. The first assay he did on the rock didn't show any values, so he tried a different process on the ore. The results of this assay showed that the ore carried fifty-two ounces of platinum to the ton. This sure got our blood to pumping, and we knew we were set for life. With that kind of ore, we knew that we would be richer than Bill Gates in just a short time. I'm sorry to say that it didn't turn out that way at all.

I've taken a lot of samples since that time, and haven't gotten an assay that showed any platinum values at all. I even had a feller named Richard Lapp, now from Wisconsin, interested in the property. He paid a friend of mine to drill several more test holes on the deposit, and do a lot more assays, and none of the assays showed any platinum at all. We didn't give old Bill Gates much of a scare after all. But I'm still collaborating with Richard Loppnow on other possible projects, and hope for the best always.

I did a lot of fence work for a feller maned LeRoy Britt over the years. He and his wife, Chook, recommended me to a lot of people for fence jobs over the years. You might say that they kept me in work for several years while I was building fence. One summer I built thirteen miles of fence for LeRoy up on the North fork of the John Day River, not too far from Ukiah. It was a good summer's job. The next year after that, a big forest fire went through that area and killed a quite a few of Le Roy's cows, and messed up a lot more of them. It also damaged the new fence I had built. It was not a good year for LeRoy and his wife.

The next spring they had leased a new pasture, and I spent the day with LeRoy going to show me the new fences I was to do maintenance on that spring. We checked out the new pasture, and went on up to where the cows had burned up, and just made a day of it.

Sometime in our conversation that day, for some reason the subject of death came up. He said that if he was going to die, that he would like to be riding a good saddle horse when it happened. He also said that he hoped that the year we were in wouldn't be as bad as the year before had been. All in all, we had a pretty good visit that day.

A week or two after our tour, I was up on the North Fork, Patching up the fence that had burned the summer before. It was about eighty miles from home, so I would spend three or four nights up there at a time. When I got home after my first trip up there, I learned that LeRoy had been killed by lightning while I was gone. I guess he was riding along on his favorite saddle horse, on an open hillside, when the lightning struck him and the horse he was riding. The fellers that found him that night said that his feet were still in the stirrups when they located him. The horse was dead, also.

LeRoy was only about sixty years old when this happened, and was about the hardest working feller I ever met. But I guess when your time is up it's up. At least he died the way he had wished to, although it was somewhat premature. We still keep in touch with his widow, Chook, after about eight or ten years. He was, she is good people.

We, as a family, have been hunting for what we call Curly Bill's treasure, for close to fifty years, off and on. I think Daddy might have learned something about the treasure as far back as 1910 or 1912, when he first left home. An old feller he worked for, named Jake Shearer, told him about some fellers borrowing a freight wagon from him back in the 1880's, when the robbery was supposed to have taken place. He said they were gone for several days, and brought the wagon back. I always wondered if that didn't have something to do with the robbery. The old man Shearer's place was about halfway between Tombstone and Skeleton Canyon, where the robbery took place. The outlaws that hid the treasure were killed just a few miles from Tombstone, or at least one of them was. The other one supposedly got away and was killed by the Indians, not too far from where we have concentrated our search over the years. There are other versions to the story, but nobody knows for sure, cause it's been so long.

My family spent a lot of time during the 1960's, through the early 1980's, looking for the treasure. I would join the fun any time I got a chance (whenever I happened to be down in that country.)

One of the last times they got serious about the treasure was sometime in the early 1980's. Marjie borrowed some hi-toned witching rods from her daughter, Debbie's boyfriend, one of the Pursley family that had lived on Frontier Road when we were young. They had a pretty good sized crew together when they went up there, including Dick and Agnes's little kids, Paula and Eric. The rods took them up a little draw to a big (thirty feet across) boulder. They pin-pointed the treasure right under that boulder. It looked like a real good place for a treasure, as the boulder was resting on one side, propped up on another big boulder, creating a cave of sorts. They made two or three trips up there, and had a good hole started under that big rock. Little Eric came face to face with a big rattlesnake that was crawling on top of a bush that was beside the rock. I guess he almost got bit, and it kinda spooked the whole crew pretty good. Anyway, they kinda gave up on the project, Most of the hunting that has been done since that time, I have done on my own. I even went back about fifteen years later, and re-dug the hole that they had been digging, to no avail. I did get a strong signal on my metal detector, but I'm sure it was a false signal. I dug to bedrock and didn't find anything.

Margie and Momma and I took a treasure hunting trip to another place two or three miles East of the "rattlesnake rock" a year or two after Daddy died in 1986. We were using a homemade witching rod this time and it pointed up the canyon that looked like it may have some possibilities. We followed that rod for what seemed like a couple miles, until we found a large area of ancient river gravel on top of a long ridge that we were on. The rod never did pinpoint anything like it was supposed to, but we did get to see a little more new country. Momma was about seventy-five years old at the time, and stayed with us most of the way. She seemed to enjoy our treasure hunting trips, and just enjoyed the outdoors, period.

After that trip, I spent a lot of time several miles Northeast of where we had been hunting. I found an area that seemed to fit the description of the treasure site we were going by. I made several trips over to that area the first year, and dug a few holes in likely looking places. I took different people over there, with better detectors that I had, but didn't find any bullion. I was being pretty careful and walking into an area where I could have driven. I wanted to keep a low profile, just in case.

The next year, I made a few more trips over there and found what I thought had to be the spot I was looking for. I did a lot of digging and detecting where I thought the treasure had to be buried.

One trip, I took my sister Bernice's boyfriend, David Dugie, with me. We spent the day digging, and detecting without any luck. This was one of the few times that I spent the night over there. We decided to spend the night and go on over to Skeleton Canyon the next day.

We got all done with our supper that night, and crawled in our bedrolls to spend the night under the stars. It seemed like I hadn't been asleep too long when David got up and started building the fire to cook breakfast. I allowed as how it seemed a little early, but he showed me his watch, and it showed that it was 6:30. We went ahead and had our breakfast, and settled back to wait for daylight. We waited quite a while and it didn't seem to be getting light. So I decided we should take another look at the Cochise County watch he had on. The watch had a picture of old Cochise on the face, and when we took a closer look, old Chief Cochise was standing on his head. We had gotten up at midnight, instead of 6:30. We turned back in, and when we woke up about daylight (6:30) there was a couple inches of snow on our bedrolls. So we decided to cut our trip short, and go on home, instead of going to Skeleton Canyon. We only had a two wheel drive rig. It was a good trip, and we've had a lot of good laughs over that midnight breakfast.

I think it was the next winter when I finally went to the rancher that controlled the access road to the area where I was doing my digging. I had found some geodes on the Forest Service land, not far from where I was digging for treasure, and used them as an excuse for being in there. I use this excuse for a year or two. We made several trips over there and I did a lot of digging. I even took Marjie over there with her witching rods. She witched a place or two, and I did a lot of digging and checking with my two-box metal detector. We never found anything, but I still thought we were in the right place.

Another year, I got a job up in Sunsites, about fifty miles from where I was raised, and spent most of the winter working for a feller named Talbot Starling. He does pump work and excavation work, and also has a nice pecan orchard up there.

He had a friend named Zane Stout that owned a trailer park there in Sunsites. One of the campers that were staying at his park was a young feller named Brett Foster, that had a nice collection of gold nuggets, that he had found with his metal detector. He had lots of nuggets that were bigger than an ounce, and he had a picture of one he had found that weighed more than fifty ounces. His picture holding that fifty-plus ounce nugget was on the Minelab metal detector ads for several years. I took Brett and several other people up to my treasure site, but nobody came up with a real good signal with their metal detectors. Brett Foster had the best detector that Minelab made at the time, but couldn't get a good signal where I was digging all my holes. We had a good trip, anyhow.

That same winter Zane Stout had an old mine over by Dragoon that he was buying from a widow-woman over there. It had a pretty good history as a gold and silver producer, and he sure wanted to see if he could get the old mine back in production. Talbot and I decided we would try to help him with the project.

We all got together one weekend day, and went over to his mine to see what we could do. There was Talbot, Zane, another young feller that was living in Sunsites at the time, and myself.

We got over to the mine and found everything was just as the previous operator had left it. The hoist and everything seemed to be in good shape. The mine shaft was about an eighty degree incline shaft, a little more than three hundred feet deep. It was timbered with a ladder and a rail-way made of four by four timbers spaced about a foot and a half apart, for the ore bucket to slide on. The ore bucket (about the size of a thirty gallon barrel) was still hanging on the hoist cable.

Talbot was our hoist man, as he had experience with his pump rig that worked on the same order. He got the hoist motor cranked up and let the ore bucket down to the bottom of the shaft, and brought it back up. Everything went smooth as silk. The kid we had with us, who claimed to be a big-time spelunker from back on the East coast, grabbed a walkie-talkie so he could communicate, and crawled in the ore bucket, and was on his way. When he got a little past the two hundred foot level, we lost contact. The shaft changed angles, and the radio waves wouldn't penetrate solid rock. When he got to the bottom and climbed out of the bucket, Talbot hoisted the bucket back up, and it was my turn to go down. I climbed in the bucket, and away I went. Things were going pretty smooth till I got just past the two hundred foot station (a platform where they got off to work a stope where they mined the ore.) When I got past the station, the track that the bucket was riding on fell out from under me, and I fell back under that station. The bucket came to rest on a six by six timber that was supposed to be holding everything in place. I knew that when the cable went slack, Talbot would hoist it up to free it, and I would be crushed on the platform up above. So I climbed out of the bucket onto the timber it was resting on. Sure enough, he hoisted the bucket back up, and when the bucket lifted off the timber I was standing on, the timber was swaying loose in the shaft. I knew I only had a few seconds of life left, and wondered how many times I would bounce before I was dead. I shined my flashlight across the shaft, and noticed the two inch pipe that had furnished compressed air to the miners. Somehow, I managed to make my way across that floating timber to that pipe, and I knew I might live another day. I know my hand-prints are still on that pipe, where I had to climb up it to get up on that station. By the time I had found that pipe, Talbot had stopped the hoist, when it came up tight under that station. He knew something was wrong, for sure. I climbed the two hundred feet up the ladder, holding on to that pipe all the way.

When I got out of that shaft, poor old Zane (who was naturally dark complected,) was as white as a sheet. He knew that at least one, maybe both of us were dead, and he blamed himself. Talbot had kinda egged him on a little, saying that he at least knew my last name, but they didn't even know the other kid's last name to put on his tombstone. Things looked a little bad for a while.

When I got to the surface and crawled out of the shaft, things looked a little better, but we still had to rescue the other kid. (I can't remember his name to save me) Zane had a detailed map to the whole mine, and it showed a stope going from the surface to the two hundred foot level, so I decided to take that route to go back down after my partner. The stope had landings about every twenty feet, which was a lot better than two hundred feet. Most of the ladders were in good shape, except the last one at the two hundred foot level. It had three or four broken rungs.

When I got back to the two hundred foot station, I was able to communicate to the kid in the bottom of the shaft, that he was going to have to climb the air pipe to get back up to where I was, cause all the timbers were dry-rotted and not usable. He started up the shaft, leaving his radio, and anything heavy in the bottom. Every time he tried to put any weight on the ladder rungs, you could hear them crack out from under him. Basically, he climbed that hundred feet on that pipe that had saved my life. We climbed back up through the stope and Zane sure was glad to see us both alive. I heard later that the kid went back a few weeks later with a safety rope, and got the radio and stuff. When we started this project, I didn't realize that it had been about fifteen years since the mine had been worked, and there had been no air circulation below the two hundred foot level. This had caused all the timbers below that level to dry-rot completely. I don't even know how the lag screws, that were holding the timber that I was standing on, even held. I guess you might say that it just wasn't my time to go, cause I had too many other adventures that needed to be took care of later on. Zane never did get his mine going.

The next year after my big mine adventure, I finally decided to let the ranch manager, where I was looking for my big treasure, know the real reason for my being over there. He was a good friend of my brother, Charlie, and I had played music with him some. He happened to be riding in one of the pastures I had to go through. I stopped to talk to him, and told him what I was really looking for up there. He asked me if I knew a certain feller over in Animas, NM. I didn't actually know the old feller, but I had played music with one of his brothers years before. He gave me this feller's name and said that he had a lot of information about the treasure I was looking for. I called the old feller and set up an appointment to meet him over on that ranch, so I could show him where I was digging for the treasure.

I met him over there on a week-end, and a young couple, that was working there at the time, went with us to my digging place. When we got there he indicated that I was not in the right place, so we went back to the ranch, and had a nice visit. In the course of our conversation, he related two or three interesting stories.

He said that when he was in his early teens, in the late 1930's and early 1940's, that he had gotten acquainted with an elderly widow-woman in Douglas, that was the aunt to Zwing Hunt, one of the outlaws that buried the Skeleton Canyon treasure. She had a map that he had supposedly drawn before he died. She offered this young feller twenty percent of the treasure if he would find it and dig it up for her. He took her up on the deal, and started the search. I guess she would just give him certain details of the map a few at a time, not letting him have unlimited access to the map. She told him to go up a certain little canyon, and dig under an over-hanging rock, a certain distance from a spring, and he would find a skeleton. He did as he was told, and sure enough, he found a skeleton, with Dobe Dollars on each eye socket. I guess it was a friend of the outlaws that they had named Davis Mountain after. She gave him other details of the map, but wouldn't show him the exact location of the treasure. Finally, he got a little frustrated, or maybe a little greedy, and decided to go it alone. One hundred percent is better than twenty percent any day. He spent a year or two in his spare time scouring them hills, to no avail, and decided he better get the widow's help. He went back to see her, and I think she had probably outsmarted him, because she had lost all of her facilities by then, and wouldn't or couldn't tell him anything at all. I don't know what happened to the map. Anyhow, I guess he tried to find that treasure every chance he got for more than fifteen years. The day I talked to him he gave me the general location, which was about twenty miles south of where I had been looking, so I changed locations for my hunt.

I spent a few days that year scouting the new area, and found most of the land-marks that were described in a couple written descriptions that I had collected by then., I knew I was finally on the right trail, after more than forty years of hunting.

The next year, during the fall of the year, I got a phone call from some feller in Sunsites that had somehow found that I was searching for that big treasure. He had some additional information that might be helpful. We got together that winter, and he took me to an old Spanish mine about eighty miles from where I was looking for my treasure, thinking that I might be looking in the wrong place. He had a map that he had gotten from the archives in Bisbee, that was supposed to be a copy of a map that Billy Grounds (the second outlaw that had buried the treasure) had given to his brother before he died. He gave me a copy of the map. Although it is a very crude copy of the map, it more or less corresponds with the description that I had got from the old man in Animas. I took this feller over to where I have been looking, but he is convinced in his mind that his location is the real thing. At least I have a map that shows the approximate location a little better now. I also got more information from the old feller in Animas that winter, including the exact location of the skeleton he dug up.

Marjie went with me with her witching rod that winter, and pin-pointed a spot pretty close to where the map says it is. I dug a pretty good hole where she said to dig, and didn't find anything. I did find a complete set of mining tools a short distance from the area we were looking, that had been left there about a hundred years before. I kinda suspect they could have belonged to the outlaws. That same winter Marjie and I collaborated with a professional treasure hunter that was living in T or C, New Mexico. He had some sophisticated equipment that was supposed to be fool-proof. It didn't locate the treasure for us. This same feller came back a couple years later with even more high-toned equipment. We were able to surround the area electronically, but not pin-point the exact spot. I still feel like we're in the right area.

One year when I was down there, we had a friend in McNeal that wanted to help us hunt our treasure. He is a Mexican, and had a set of Spanish dip-needles that were guaranteed fool-proof. They had been blessed by the Pope back in the 1700's, and had been handed down in his family for two or three hundred years, Supposedly, the Spaniards used dip-needles to find all the rich mines in the Southwest. Anyway, it sure was worth a try. I took the feller, his son and son's girlfriend over to my treasure area to try out his dip-needles. He and his son did their little "Hail Mary," or some kind of silent prayer, and away we went. To make them needles work, two people stand facing each other with a needle in each hand, and touch the needles together. If they are parallel to a treasure or rich ore vein, the needles will swing toward it. On their initial try the needles swung in the general direction of my treasure site, so I felt pretty good. We went on for a couple miles, stopping every quarter mile or so, to check, and they kept swinging the right way. We finally got to where Marjie and I had been looking, and the needles kept pointing up the hill. We missed my spot by a couple hundred yards. Finally we got to the foot of a real steep hill, and by then the old man was too tired to go on, so we decided to come back in a day or two.

We came back a day or two later, and Margie took the old man's place, cause he was too stove up to make the trip. I couldn't take his place because I'm a life-long heathen, and couldn't do the fancy prayer business that makes them needles work. When we got to where we had left off on our last trip, I went on ahead of the crew to check out some caves that I could see under the cliffs at the top of the hill we were climbing. (The old man from Animas had told me that someone had found about a dozen pack saddles in a cave in that area back in the 30's or 40's.) I checked out several caves that day, but never found anything.

I spent a quite a while looking through several small caves under the rim-rocks, and went to check on the rest of the crew. They were just getting up to the foot of the cliffs, as it was a real steep hill. We sat down and had out lunch, and when we got back up and checked their dip-needles, they pointed back down the hill. We went down the hill a couple hundred feet, to a fifty foot square boulder, and the needles pointed down towards the ground, which indicated the treasure was buried there. Margie took her witching rod, and it bounced eight or nine times, indicating the treasure was eight or nine feet down. We were finally rich! All we had to do was dig it up.

About this time, I took a little time off to entertain a couple of friends from Oregon for a few days. Jim Doherty, and a feller named Frank Burns came to visit for a few days, and I took them around to some of the places that I like down there. We went to the big Indian artifacts museum up at Dragoon, and came back around the circle through Benson, Tombstone and Bisbee. One day we gathered up a big crew, including my sisters, Bernice and Margie, and the old man and his son and son's girlfriend (with the dip-needles) and went to Skeleton Canyon to see if we could find some loose coins where the big robbery had taken place. We didn't find any coins, but found a few artifacts and had a good trip. On our way home, I took Jim and Frank to Mud Springs where there are a lot of Indian painting, and some ruins of old villages. On another trip, we got to chase a javelina for a little ways with my car. I think I showed them boys a good time that week.

The next week-end I decided to go back up and see if I could dig up the treasure we had located. I took the Old man's son with me so he could help carry their share of that treasure. I would have been a little skeptical of our big find, except for the story about the pack-saddles. That had made me think it might have been possible to get pack mules to where we were going. Besides, them dip-needles were supposed to be fool-proof. We came at the area from a different area because I had been getting red-tagged some days where I had been parking close to the highway. We intended to stay at least one night. We got to our trail-head and I loaded all the heavy stuff in my pack and carried the pick and shovel besides. I was in pretty good shape at the time. We loaded the young feller as light as we could, and headed up the hill. It was probably three miles to our treasure. When we got a mile or more up the canyon, I saw some caves I wanted to explore, so I left the kid on the trail and climbed up the hill to explore the caves. I was quite a ways up the hillside, heading parallel to the trail. One of the caves had some wet-back stuff in it, but nothing that could be linked to the treasure, It had been a good idea to look, anyhow. I went side-hill for the rest of the way to our treasure, and when I got there I unloaded my pack and went back a half mile or so, and took the kid's pack and carried it the rest of the way. He had a hard time climbing the steep part of the hill without the pack. We used up most of that day getting up to the treasure, but I did dig a little that evening. We built us a good fire, and ate a bite, and settled in for the night at the bottom of the big cliffs.

The next morning we got up and had breakfast, and went to digging on our treasure. I took time to check our hole out about every three or four feet, with my metal detector. We spent a good part of that day digging and checking, but never came up with a good signal, so after we got down to nine or ten feet, we decided it was a false alarm. We loaded up for the trip out. I took off in the lead, intending to go to the car and come back to help the kid with his pack. When I located him, he had lost his bedroll, and was pretty tuckered out. I guess the bedroll had gotten away from him on the steep part of the hill, and he just watched it roll away down the hill. I guess that it is still there. We had a good trip, even if it wasn't too profitable. That was the last time I saw that family, though. I think they might still be living down there. I lost my faith in them Spanish dip-needles after that.

Since that trip, I have concentrated my efforts in the area where Margie and I first started hunting, not too far from where I found the mining tools.

One winter I spent about ten days digging near a rock that I thought might be a marker for the treasure. I kept getting a signal, but it turned out to be a false signal, caused by the ground moisture.

Another winter, I found a rock that I thought might have been the marker rock for the treasure. That was my last trip up there for the season, and I was in a hurry that day, so I just marked the spot in my mind. I didn't put up any real markers, because I knew I could go right back to the spot. I have been back to that area more than a dozen times since that day, and have taken several other people there over the years, and no-one has been able to find that rock again. I've started calling it my "phantom rock."

While I was visiting with the ranch manager that lined me up with the old feller in Animas, he related an interesting story that is worth telling. It seems like one of his relatives (I think it was his daddy's uncle) had a small ranch over in New Mexico back in the 1930's and 1940's. I guess the old feller was a bachelor, and was not too generous with his money. He did his business in cash, not using the banks. They figured he should have had a little money put away when he died, I guess they searched his house pretty good after he died, and didn't find too much money. They went on and sold his ranch to settle his estate. The old cabin that he had lived in didn't amount to much, so the new owner tore it down to build something better. When they took the floor out they found a hole in the floor with a gallon bucket underneath it. I guess the bucket was almost full of gold and silver coins that he old feller had dropped through that hole in the floor. There was more than enough value in them coins to pay for the ranch. They offered to split the money with the estate of the old man, but they refused it. I guess they figured a deal was a deal. That's what I consider good people.

I have taken several people to my treasure site in the last ten years. One day I took Raymond McCormick, a lifetime friend of my family. We had a nice relaxing trip with his hiking around the area while I checked out a place or two to dig. During the day, he suggested to me that probably the best way to make any money hunting treasure was to write a story about my treasure hunting trips. I hope that some of what I have written will be interesting to somebody in this old world.

Not too many years ago, I took a geologist from back in the mid-west up to my treasure site. We spent the day up there, and located what we thought to be an unmarked grave. This find corresponded with the information that

I have gathered over the years of searching for the treasure. The outlaws supposedly killed a feller that helped them bury the treasure. I assume that they would have buried the body, to keep the buzzards from attracting attention to the area. We marked the spot and checked it with our metal detectors, but didn't find any metal at the time. The geologist did point out some interesting mineralized ground on our way back to our rig. He thought this ground might be worth more than the thirty million dollar treasure we were hunting. He took a few samples to get them assayed, but I never learned the results of the assays.

The winter of 2004-2005, I took my grandson, Jonathon, to Southeastern Arizona. We stopped in Littleton, Colorado for a week, at our youngest son, David's home. He and his wife, Bridget, showed us a good time, including attending a Denver Nuggets basketball game. We spent Christmas week there.

In Arizona, I took Jonathon over to the treasure site. He had heard us talk about the treasure quite a bit, over the years, and thought that he and I could just go down there and dig it up. We dug some on the grave I had found the year before, but didn't find any bones. We may not have been deep enough. I hope to go back some day and do some more digging and checking in that area. I still think I am in the right area. I don't think I'll do anything over this year, but hope to get back over next winter, if things go about half right. I hope Jon had a good trip to remember.

I have filed on some mining claims in this Huntington, Oregon area, and hope to promote them to some kind of production this coming summer. The precious metals prices are coming up all the time, so maybe we can get something going. I guess you might say that it's another rainbow to chase.

Sincerely,
"Arizona" W. D. Kennedy
The rainbow chaser

00461286O